# INVINCIBLE
## 2012 BAYLOR LADY BEARS
## NCAA® CHAMPIONS

**JENNIFER REISS HANNAH**

EDITOR

WITH PHOTOGRAPHS BY
**ROBERT ROGERS**

BIG BEAR BOOKS
AN IMPRINT OF BAYLOR UNIVERSITY PRESS

*Cover and Interior Design* by *the*BookDesigners
*Cover Image* by Robert Rogers

*Photo Credits:* Photography by Robert Rogers and Matthew Minard/Baylor
Marketing & Communications, unless otherwise noted below.

• Associated Press: Pages 16, 19

• Isaac Dovalina/*Round Up* Photographer: Pages 70, 71

• Meagan Downing/*Lariat* Photographer: Pages 42, 61

• Ryan Duncan/Baylor Marketing & Communications: Page 8

• Matt Hellman /*Lariat* Photo Editor: Pages 17, 20, 68, 69, 72, 73

• Makenzie Mason/*Lariat* Photographer: Page 42

•Matthew McCarroll/*Lariat* Photographer: Page 61


Thanks also to Ariadne Aberin for her assistance and contributions.


Big Bear Books is an imprint of Baylor University Press.
This book has been catalogued with the Library of Congress under ISBN
978-1-60258-673-4.

BAYLOR ®
U N I V E R S I T Y
Printed in the United States of America on acid-free paper.

nament, defeated during the Elite Eight round by rival Texas A&M. Instead of brushing aside their discontent, Coach Kim Mulkey and her team embraced the setback, using it as motivation to push through the 2011-12 season while focusing solely on the 2012 national title.

And motivating it was. National headlines told the story of a team on a mission, polishing their game throughout regular season play to prepare themselves for an ultimate victory. The Lady Bears crushed, stampeded, derailed, their path. They dominated offensively and defensively, utilizing each player's talent for win after win.

Along the way to becoming national champions, the Lady Bears achieved a historic milestone by becoming the first NCAA Division I basketball team ever to attain a 40-0 season record—but that was never their intention. A perfect season was simply the byproduct of the team's sheer focus on completing the task at hand: to finish what they started. It was a magical season for a team UNBEATABLE, UNSHAKABLE, INVINCIBLE.

| NO. | NAME | POS | YEAR |
|---|---|---|---|
| 22 | Sune Agbuke | P | FR |
| 44 | Mariah Chandler | P/F | JR |
| 20 | Terran Condrey | G | SR |
| 24 | Ashley Field | P | SR |
| 42 | Brittney Griner | P | JR |
| 1 | Kimetria Hayden | G | JR |
| 3 | Jordan Madden | G | JR |
| 25 | Lindsay Palmer | G | SR |
| 32 | Brooklyn Pope | F/P | RS JR |
| 14 | Makenzie Robertson | G | SO |
| 0 | Odyssey Sims | G | SO |
| 4 | Shanay Washington | G | RS SO |
| 10 | Destiny Williams | F/P | RS JR |

# BAYLOR 82 VS. HOWARD 28

Friday, Nov. 11, 2011, 6:30 p.m. CT
Ferrell Center, Waco
Attendance: 7,587

## LOOKING BACK, MOVING FORWARD

Pregame activities set the tone for the new season, serving as a reminder of the prior season's accomplishments and, ultimately, its shortcoming. Baylor University unveiled three new banners in the Ferrell Center, representing the 2010-2011 Lady Bears' regular season Big 12 Championship, their Big 12 Tournament Championship, and their Elite Eight appearance. The pregame video featured Coach Kim Mulkey in a preseason locker room pep talk, challenging her team to reach the ultimate prize—the one they failed to grasp last year—the national championship.

Fans came to see the Lady Bears strut their stuff for the record after the team had swept two exhibition games. Everyone in the Ferrell Center expected the No. 1 Lady Bears to defeat Howard University in the first round of the Preseason Women's National Invitation Tournament; the only question was by how much. Though a bit rusty, Baylor notched a lopsided win against a team that finished the previous season 16-18 and was second place in the Mid-Eastern Athletic Conference Tournament.

- Baylor outscored Howard 48-12 in the paint.

- The Lady Bears held the Howard Bison to 16 percent shooting, hitting only 1 out of 18 tries from three-point range. Baylor had not allowed an opponent to shoot more than 50 percent since March 2006.

- Junior center Brittney Griner put up 22 points, 13 rebounds, and 8 blocks in her 27th career double-double.

- Sophomore guard Odyssey Sims racked up 15 points in the 24th double-digit scoring game of her career.

- Baylor increased their nonconference Ferrell Center winning streak to 48 games.

- The Lady Bears are 12-0 in Ferrell Center season openers under Kim Mulkey.

# BAYLOR 91 VS. CHATTANOOGA 31

Sunday, Nov. 13, 2011, 2 p.m. CT
Ferrell Center, Waco
Attendance: 7,005

## A MILESTONE FOR MULKEY

Coach Kim Mulkey notched her 300th career win as a head coach with a victory over Chattanooga in the second round of the WNIT. She came into the game with a .791 career-winning percentage—ranking fourth nationally—while Chattanooga coach Wes Moore ranked seventh with a .767 percentage. Mulkey's entire 12-year head coaching career has been at Baylor. Her arrival at the 300-win mark was the quickest in women's basketball history.

"That's a reflection of the kids you coach," Mulkey said of the milestone. "I know my name goes by it, but truthfully it's just wins for our program. It's a reflection of the great players I've been allowed to coach. It's also a reflection of the university I work for, in that it's important that they allow me to go out and hire good assistant coaches."

After the players lifted a reluctant Mulkey onto their shoulders, the coach said, "This team, I can't stay mad at them long. How do you fight them coming to lift you? And you know what? I could lift them up, because they've got a lot more wins left in this basketball team."

Mulkey said her team played with more intensity and energy than they had two days earlier. Chattanooga scored the first bucket, but the Lady Bears answered with a 19-0 run and never looked back.

STATS, STARS, AND STREAKS

- Mulkey's career record stands at 300-79, with eight straight NCAA tournament trips.
- Odyssey Sims outscored Chattanooga by herself in the first half—16 to their 12.
- Freshman Sune Agbuke got some time on the court and pulled in 10 rebounds.
- Brooklyn Pope earned a double-double with 16 points and 10 rebounds.
- Terran Condrey and Jordan Madden hit career highs in assists, with eight and seven respectively.
- Chattanooga's 31 points were that team's fewest ever in a game.
- Brittney Griner made her 400th career block during the match.

# KIM MULKEY

POSITION: Head Coach
HOMETOWN: Hammond, La.
ALMA MATER: Louisiana Tech

During her 12 years as Lady Bears Head Coach, Kim Mulkey has transformed Baylor women's basketball into one of the nation's elite programs. The Women's Basketball Hall of Famer guided the Lady Bears this season to their second NCAA national championship and an unprecedented 40-0 season record, making the Lady Bears the first women's basketball team in NCAA history to do so. Mulkey attained her 300th career victory during the match against Chattanooga on Nov. 13, 2011, ranking her No. 4 among the winningest active women's basketball Division I head coaches. She finished the season with an impressive 335-79 Baylor career record, averaging 27.8 wins a season. Baylor ranks No. 5 among the NCAA Division I's winningest teams over the 12-year span of Mulkey's reign.

This year the former Olympic Gold medalist added the following awards to her long list of honors: the Naismith Women's College Coach of the Year, the Russell Athletic/Women's Basketball Coaches Association (WBCA) Coach of the Year, The Associated Press Coach of the Year, the Big 12 Conference Coach of the Year, and the WBCA Region 5 Coach of the Year.

Since stepping into her role as head coach on Apr. 4, 2000, Mulkey has produced amazing results. In winning the 2005 title she became the first person, man or woman, to win a basketball national championship as a player, assistant coach, and head coach. In addition to two national championships, under Mulkey's leadership the Lady Bears program has achieved 11 NCAA tournament appearances, and 7 Big 12 Conference titles.

Mulkey has always had a strong inclination toward athletics. As a child she played baseball, and upon beginning high school, Mulkey decided to concentrate on basketball. Mulkey continued her basketball career at Louisiana Tech, first as a college player and then in the roles of assistant coach and associate head coach. She was a member of the gold-medal-winning U.S. Women's Basketball team in the 1984 Summer Olympics held in Los Angeles, Calif., coached by Pat Summitt.

# BAYLOR 83 VS. UCLA 50

Thursday, Nov. 17, 2011, 7 p.m.
Ferrell Center, Waco
Attendance: 7,577

## BAYLOR DEFEATS FIRST RANKED OPPONENT

Baylor faced its first ranked team in a match-up with No. 22 UCLA in the third round of the preseason WNIT.

Defense was key to the victory that did not look at all certain in the first half. During one stretch, UCLA went on an 8-0 run, and the Lady Bears found themselves ahead only 27-23 with 28 seconds left in the first half. That's when guard Odyssey Sims made her move. She held the ball in the backcourt while the clock ticked, then drove for a layup with 4.8 seconds remaining, drew the foul, and made the free throw. The score was 30-23 at the half.

Baylor quickly sealed the fate of the game with a 30-2 run after halftime. With 18 points, Brittney Griner scored in double figures for her 43rd straight game. Destiny Williams scored 16 points, making UCLA pay for double-teaming Griner in the paint. Kimetria "Nae-Nae" Hayden scored 10 points off the bench and added 5 assists.

Coach Kim Mulkey said, "Your defense can be special for you. It was a great example for them, to see what I've been trying to tell them. If they'll just commit to being the best defensive team, I think they'll understand that, hey, you finally hung in there long enough to extend the lead."

Mulkey said that better rebounding and penetrating to draw fouls were the keys to the improved second half in which Baylor outscored UCLA 53-27.

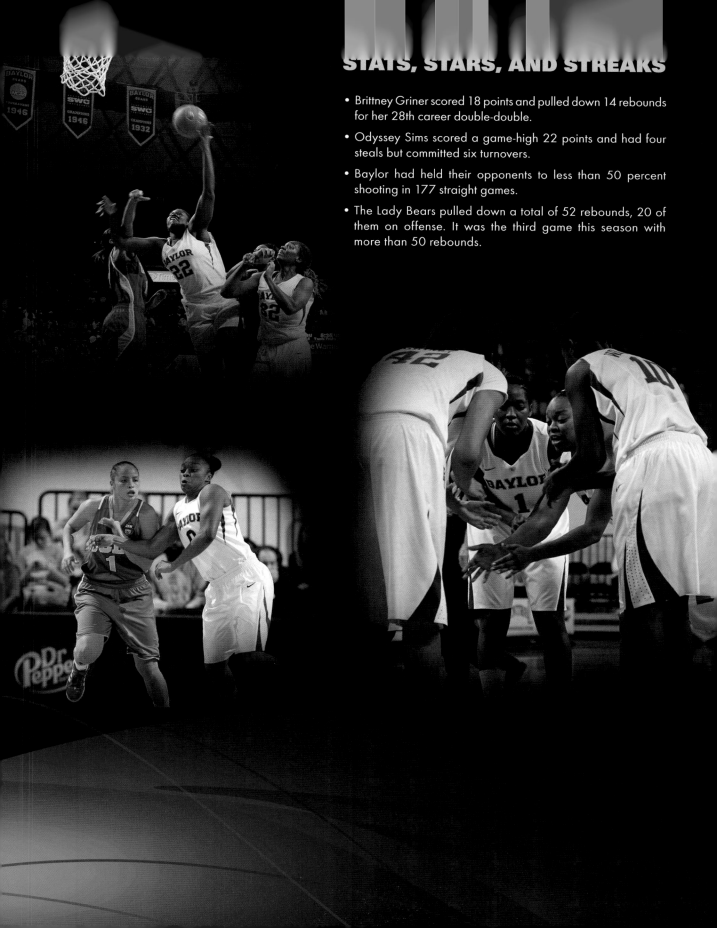

# STATS, STARS, AND STREAKS

- Brittney Griner scored 18 points and pulled down 14 rebounds for her 28th career double-double.

- Odyssey Sims scored a game-high 22 points and had four steals but committed six turnovers.

- Baylor had held their opponents to less than 50 percent shooting in 177 straight games.

- The Lady Bears pulled down a total of 52 rebounds, 20 of them on offense. It was the third game this season with more than 50 rebounds.

# BAYLOR 94 VS. NOTRE DAME 81

Sunday, Nov. 20, 2011, 1 p.m. CT
Ferrell Center, Waco
Attendance: 9,477

## LADY BEARS ACE THEIR FIRST TRUE TEST

The No. 1 Lady Bears won their first WNIT preseason tournament championship with a defeat of No. 2-ranked Notre Dame. The Fighting Irish claim some of the nation's top players, including guard Skylar Diggins, who was named a preseason top five player in the country.

Junior post Brittney Griner led the scoring with 32 points and pulled in 14 rebounds in the Lady Bears' first televised game of the season.

"I was really pumped," said Griner, who noted before the game that she was looking forward to the challenge.

Notre Dame Coach Muffet McGraw said after the game, "We expected coming in that [Griner] was going to be able to have her way inside, and we tried a couple of different looks on her, but it didn't really matter. She's an incredibly talented young lady."

Despite Griner's dominance, Coach Kim Mulkey noted, "We're not just a one-player team. You look down the lineup, and we're pretty darn good." Baylor's 32 points off the bench proved Mulkey's point. Notre Dame earned only five points from bench players. Odyssey Sims (25) and Destiny Williams (15) also scored in double digits.

Free throws were pivotal, too, with Baylor scoring 29 off 38 trips to the line. The Lady Bears grabbed 20 offensive rebounds, leading to 21 second-chance points.

Going up against Diggins was a big test for Baylor's Sims, who drew a technical foul in a mid-court dust-up with Diggins. But Sims was fierce on defense, recording a career-high six steals.

# STATS, STARS, AND STREAKS

- Griner blocked 22 shots in the WNIT, breaking the previous record of 20, set by Lady Bear Danielle Wilson in 2006.
- Terran Condrey had a career-high five steals.
- Attendance was the fourth largest this season.
- The Lady Bears held an opponent to under 50 percent shooting for 178 games in a row

# BAYLOR 109 VS. YALE 59

Tuesday, Nov. 22, 2011, 6:30 p.m. CT
Ferrell Center, Waco
Attendance: 7,681

## SLOW START, BIG WIN

Two days after taking down No. 2 Notre Dame and winning the Preseason WNIT, the Lady Bears came out with a sluggish start against Yale. Coach Kim Mulkey pulled her entire starting lineup only a few minutes into the game because they were trailing behind.

"We just couldn't get going," commented Mulkey. "I made a substitution and I was very proud of the five kids that came in the game."

The team had not practiced the day before so that Mulkey and her staff could attend the memorial service for the Oklahoma State coaches who were killed in a plane crash the week prior.

The early substitutions snapped players back to attention, and three Lady Bears—Big 12's Player of the Week Brittney Griner, Odyssey Sims, and Brooklyn Pope—each finished with a double-double. The Lady Bears outrebounded Yale 52-23 and ended with a 109-59 victory.

"Believe it or not, we think that was kind of fun," Bulldogs coach Chris Gobrecht said. "At Yale, we live in a really different world. So it's a neat thing for us as coaches and players to step into a place that is all about women's basketball. It's so different from the life that we all live."

- All Baylor players who entered the game tallied points. This had not happened since a December 2010 game against UT-Pan American.

- Baylor's score of 109 points were the most since scoring 117 points against Sam Houston State on Dec. 4, 2006.

- Double-doubles from Griner, Sims, and Pope marked the first time three players have done so since Nov. 29, 2007 against Southeast Missouri.

- The Lady Bears held an opponent to under 50 percent shooting for 179 straight games.

# BRITTNEY GRINER
## #42

POSITION: Post
CLASS: Junior
HEIGHT: 6' 8"
HOMETOWN: Houston, Tex.

Notorious for her exceptional talent and unparalleled feats of athleticism, Brittney Griner has quickly become the most recognizable name in women's basketball. Averaging 23.2 points, 9.4 rebounds, and 5.2 blocks per game, Griner led the Lady Bears to their second national championship title in seven years. She became the second Lady Bear in Baylor history to be named the Most Outstanding Player of the national tournament.

The 6-foot-8-inch phenom is transforming women's basketball one block, one rebound, one slam at a time. With a 7-foot-4-inch wingspan and a 9-foot-2-inch vertical reach, the junior post's defensive presence on the court forces her opponents to change their approach to the game and has been formally dubbed the Griner Effect. Challengers have attempted multiple strategies to overcome the Effect, but none have proven successful enough to defeat Griner and the Baylor squad.

The ESPN.com National Player of the Year, Griner broke national records and set new career highs this season. She currently holds the Big 12 Conference career block record and ranks No. 2 on the NCAA Division I career block list. Her 2,000th point scored on Feb. 4 against Kansas State made her the only NCAA basketball player, male or female, to score 2,000 points and block 500 shots. On Mar. 9, Griner, the only collegiate finalist for the 2012 U.S. Olympic Team, set a career high 45 points against Kansas State.

Griner's stellar performance garnered numerous accolades this season. She earned multiple player-of-the-year honors, including The Associated Press Player of the Year; the 2012 Naismith Trophy for Women's College Player of the Year, regarded as the most prestigious national basketball award; and the State Farm Wade Trophy, considered "The Heisman of Women's Basketball." Griner received All-American status from The Associated Press, the Women's Basketball Coaches Association, and the U.S. Basketball Writers Association. In addition to receiving the Wooden Award, she was named most outstanding player of the Des Moines Regional and the Big 12 Championship, Big 12 Player of the Year, Big 12 Defensive Player of the Year, and Big 12 Player of the Week seven times.

The health, human performance, and recreation major with an outdoor recreation emphasis aspires to play professional basketball upon graduation.

# BAYLOR 76 VS. TENNESSEE 67

Sunday, Nov. 27, 2011, 1 p.m. CT
Thompson-Boling Arena, Knoxville, Tenn.
Attendance: 16,623

## VICTORY OVER THE VOLS

The No. 1 Lady Bears faced tough competition on the court in Knoxville, Tenn., against Pat Summitt's No. 7 Lady Volunteers.

The Lady Vols defense contained Brittney Griner in the first half and challenged her teammates to step up their performance if they desired a win. Tennessee sent Kim Mulkey's team to the locker room trailing 31-33 at the half. Baylor had surrendered 18 offensive rebounds and made the necessary adjustments the second half to take down Tennessee 76-67.

Griner found her rhythm and scored 17 of her 26 points after the break. Odyssey Sims totaled 23 points and Jordan Madden added 11 points.

"We took their best shot," Mulkey said. "How many games are you going to get outrebounded as much as we did, particularly on the offensive end, and win?"

"Baylor is a great team, and I don't think we'll see one any better," Summitt said.

Baylor had beaten Tennessee in three consecutive seasons, despite the Lady Vols holding the rebounding advantage in each of those games.

## STATS, STARS, AND STREAKS

- This game was Baylor's first win in Knoxville.
- The win for the Lady Bears put an end to Tennessee's 38-game home winning streak, dating back to a Feb. 16, 2009, loss to Duke.
- Odyssey Sims recorded the 29th double-digit scoring performance of her career and sixth of the year.
- Jordan Madden reached career highs with 3 blocks and 38 minutes of playing time while recording double-figure points for the eighth time in her career.
- Both teams sported "We Back Pat" warm-up shirts before the game in support of Summitt, who announced in August 2011 that she had been diagnosed with early onset dementia.

# BAYLOR 91 VS. TEXAS SOUTHERN 39

Wednesday, Nov. 30, 2011, 7 p.m. CT
Ferrell Center, Waco
Attendance: 7,048

## A CAKEWALK FOR BAYLOR

Returning to Waco from a victorious road trip to Tennessee, top-ranked Baylor continued their home winning streak with a lopsided 91-39 win over nonranked Texas Southern.

The Lady Bears opened up a 20-point lead early on, allowing Coach Kim Mulkey to substitute the team's reserve players throughout the game. Baylor used the opportunity as they would a team practice, to prepare for more challenging contests to come.

"We just try to do what [Mulkey] asks us to do without her having to ask us to do it," said Brooklyn Pope. "It's kind of like a pop quiz, preparing us for the test when we play someone a little bit tougher."

"We didn't look at the opponent, we didn't look at the scoreboard," commented Mulkey. "[It was] an opportunity to come home after a big victory on the road and just play. Everybody got to play."

The Lady Tigers faced an unbalanced matchup from the start. Texas Southern started three freshmen while Baylor's lineup included a senior, three juniors, and a sophomore. Texas Southern finished with 31 turnovers that led to 43 Baylor points and another win for the Lady Bears.

# STATS, STARS, AND STREAKS

- Brittney Griner had 23 points and 14 rebounds for her fifth double-double this season.
- Odyssey Sims had 19 points, 9 assists and a career-high 8 steals.
- Kimetria Hayden and Brooklyn Pope had 13 points apiece.
- Sune Agbuke had career highs in blocks (5) and assists (2).
- Pope recorded the 11th double-figure scoring game of her career and third of the season with 13 points.
- With four rebounds, Makenzie Robertson tied her career high.

# TERRAN CONDREY
## #20

**POSITION:** Guard
**CLASS:** Senior
**HEIGHT:** 5′ 7″
**HOMETOWN:** Eufaula, Ala.

Terran Condrey is known by her teammates as a valuable, dependable Lady Bear. A senior health, human performance, and recreation major set to graduate in May 2012, Condrey made crucial shots during critical moments. Her record speaks for itself. During the Feb. 18 match against Texas Tech, Condrey scored a 3-pointer that triggered Baylor's comeback and ultimate victory. She made another pivotal 3-pointer that helped push Baylor back into the lead and claim a win against Oklahoma on Jan. 26.

"I've coached a lot of great players, I've coached a lot of great kids," head coach Kim Mulkey said. "They don't get any better than Terran Condrey ... She's low-maintenance, she's respectful. She will go down as one of my all-time favorite kids."

Away from the court Condrey might be found polishing her pool game or heading to the movie theater. Upon graduation she plans on playing basketball overseas and attending graduate school. With her involvement in helping the Lady Bears earn a perfect regular season, Condrey will be a name not soon forgotten.

# STATS, STARS, AND STREAKS

- Baylor marked its 700th program victory.
- Griner reached 434 career blocks, bringing her closer to OU's Courtney Paris' Big 12 record of 446.
- Odyssey Sims (15 points) recorded the 31st double-digit score of her career and eighth of the year. She also added nine assists and four steals.
- Kimetria Hayden scored 11 points, her third double-digit scoring performance of the season and 16th of her career.
- On Dec. 1, Griner and Sims were two of seven Big 12 women's basketball players to be placed on the Naismith Trophy Early Season Watch List.

## BAYLOR 89 VS. MINNESOTA 60

Sunday, Dec. 4, 2011, 1 p.m. CT
Williams Arena, Minneapolis, Minn.
Attendance: 3,814

### GOPHERS NO CONTEST FOR THE LADY BEARS

The Lady Bears continued their journey toward the NCAA championship with a Big 12/Big Ten challenge in Minneapolis against the Gophers.

Baylor started strong with a 27-point lead at the break but became somewhat complacent after halftime. Though the match ended in a 29-point win for her team, Coach Kim Mulkey saw much room for improvement.

"I really don't think we played very well," said Mulkey. "I thought we turned the ball over way too many times and gave away too many gimme buckets. ... I just didn't see the same focus that we are going to have to have to win a championship."

Brittney Griner reached the 20-point mark for the fifth consecutive game and made nine rebounds. She has become comfortable attracting multiple defenders.

"I'm used to having two or three players on me. To me that's like a one-on-one now," said Griner. "I just have to be patient and find my players."

# BAYLOR 72 VS. MILWAUKEE 41

Thursday, Dec. 8, 2011, 7 p.m. CT
Ferrell Center, Waco
Attendance: 7,066

## SHOW-STOPPING SIMS

Sophomore Odyssey Sims has proven she is a stable force on the court alongside star teammate Brittney Griner. In the matchup against Wisconsin-Milwaukee, Sims carried the game for several stretches with impressive offensive and defensive skills.

"Odyssey Sims has come to play in the last month, " said Coach Kim Mulkey. "It is enjoyable to watch her. When we tip off, she is ready to play."

With a combined 57 points Lady Bears trio Sims, Griner, and Pope outscored Milwaukee on their own. Together Griner and Sims held a 16-2 run for Baylor, increasing the Lady Bears' lead by 15 points only 13 minutes into the game. The first ever matchup between the schools ended in a 72-41 Baylor victory against Milwaukee.

"Their athleticism, and their aggressiveness, they just took us out of our offense…," said Milwaukee Coach Sandy Botham. "They are the best team in the country."

## STATS, STARS, AND STREAKS

- This game marked a 54-game home nonconference win streak and a 28th consecutive home win for Baylor.

- Sims registered the 32nd double-digit scoring performance of her career and ninth of the year.

- Brittney Griner (20 points) scored in double figures in 49 straight games and in 79 of 81 in her career. Griner's total left her just two points shy of No. 7 on the all-time Baylor scoring charts.

- Brooklyn Pope recorded a season-high 18 points and 11 rebounds, her third double-double of the year and eighth of her career.

# STATS, STARS, AND STREAKS

- Baylor is 2-0 in Maggie Dixon Classic games.
- Baylor had 87 consecutive games scoring 70 or more points.
- With 1,724 points, Brittney Griner moved to No. 6 on the Baylor career scoring chart, passing LaNita Luckey's (1988-92) 1,721.
- Playing a career-high 40 minutes, Jordan Madden (11 points) scored in double figures for the third time this season.

# BAYLOR 73 VS. ST. JOHN'S 59

Sunday, Dec. 11, 2011, 12 p.m. CT
Madison Square Garden, New York
Attendance: 5,486

## BAYLOR TAKES A BITE OF THE BIG APPLE

Baylor University celebrated an exceptional weekend in New York City with the crowning of Heisman Trophy winner Robert Griffin III and the Lady Bears' defeat of St. John's in the Maggie Dixon Classic. The Lady Bears gathered outside of the Heisman ceremony site to support their classmate and proceeded on to a Broadway show, during which they received word of his triumph by text message.

Unfortunately their performance the following morning was nowhere near as electrifying as their previous evening's stage entertainment. Baylor looked shaky during the first half. St. John's put up a strong defense against Griner to keep her from the ball, and Odyssey Sims had difficulty finding the bucket, missing all four of her first-half shots.

The Lady Bears trailed 36-30 early in the second half but finally found their stride to beat St. John's 73-59.

"Today would have been the perfect environment to get beat," said Coach Kim Mulkey. "We had a lot of things distracting us, let alone the opponent we were playing."

# BAYLOR 66 VS. CONNECTICUT 61

Sunday, Dec. 18, 2011, 7:30 pm CT
Ferrell Center, Waco
Attendance: 10,627

## BATTLING TO REMAIN NO. 1

The Baylor-Connecticut clash set records even before a single player stepped onto the court. Weeks prior to the highly anticipated game pitting the No. 1 and No. 2 teams in the country, the Lady Bears achieved an advance sellout for the first time in program history.

Last year the rankings were reversed as No. 1 UConn took on No. 2 Baylor in Hartford, Conn. Brittney Griner's less-than-exceptional free throw performance and Odyssey Sims' last-chance half-court net-missing heave contributed to Baylor's 65-64 defeat. But the Lady Bears were prepared for the rematch on their home territory.

Though both teams entered the game after a break for semester finals, their play was not hampered. Griner's free throws were flawless. She netted all seven attempts, six of which occurred during Baylor's 27-11 spurt near the end. Griner's nine blocks broke the Big 12 career record and landed her in fourth place on the NCAA all-time career blocks list.

UConn led 34-28 at halftime and increased the margin to 11 points within five minutes after the break. But Baylor fought back and, with a key 3-pointer by Terran Condrey and four free throws by Sims, sealed a win for the Lady Bears with a final score of 66-61.

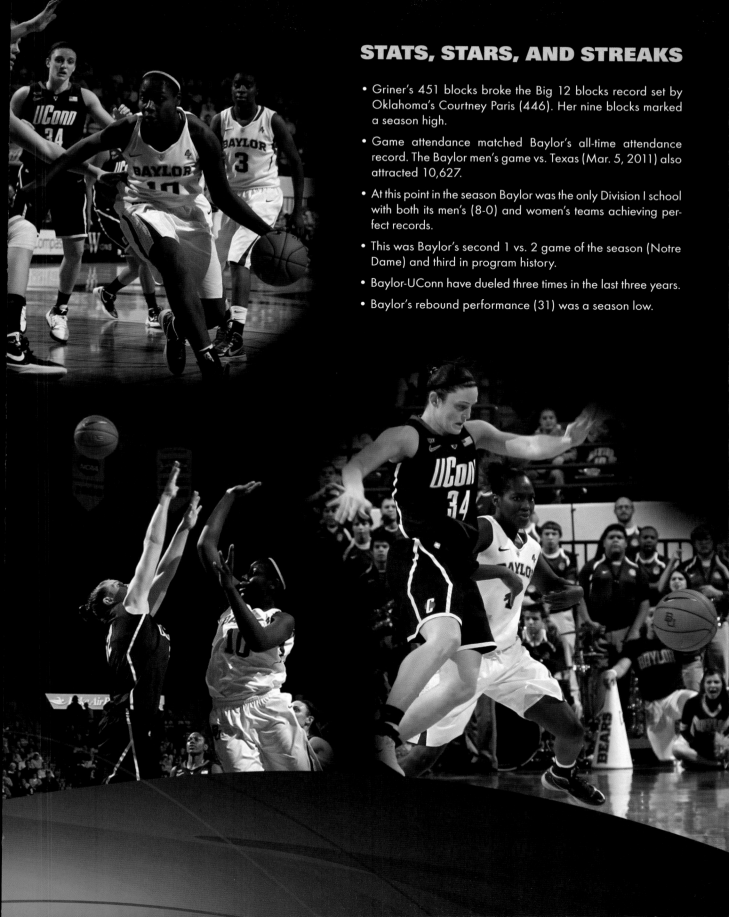

# STATS, STARS, AND STREAKS

- Griner's 451 blocks broke the Big 12 blocks record set by Oklahoma's Courtney Paris (446). Her nine blocks marked a season high.

- Game attendance matched Baylor's all-time attendance record. The Baylor men's game vs. Texas (Mar. 5, 2011) also attracted 10,627.

- At this point in the season Baylor was the only Division I school with both its men's (8-0) and women's teams achieving perfect records.

- This was Baylor's second 1 vs. 2 game of the season (Notre Dame) and third in program history.

- Baylor-UConn have dueled three times in the last three years.

- Baylor's rebound performance (31) was a season low.

# ASHLEY FIELD
# #24

POSITION: Post
CLASS: Senior
HEIGHT: 6' 2"
HOMETOWN: Burnet, Tex.

Ashley Field has been recognized multiple times for her dedication and exceptional performance in both her academic and basketball careers. Field graduated with a degree in health, human performance, and recreation in December 2011 and is pursuing a post-baccalaureate degree in speech communication. February marked Field's second Academic All-Big 12 first team honor; she first received conference recognition in 2010.

Regarded by Coach Kim Mulkey as a low-maintenance player, Field played a critical role for the Lady Bears behind the scenes. Field pushed her teammates toward excellence during practices and selflessly bore the bruises from guarding Brittney Griner. Going into the NCAA tournament Field led the Lady Bears in 3-point field goal percentage (.600). Field was one of the six Lady Bears who scored double figures during the McNeese State game on Dec. 21, 2011, and registered another double-figure score—the 17th of her career—nine days later against Mississippi Valley State.

Field chose to attend Baylor over Texas Tech, Iowa, and West Virginia because of her desire to play in the Big 12 and because of the honor of playing for one of the sport's all-time greatest coaches.

# STATS, STARS, AND STREAKS

- Six players scored in double figures: Brittney Griner (15), Sune Agbuke (10), Odyssey Sims (16), Kimetria Hayden (15), Destiny Williams (13), and Ashley Field (10). Previous occurrence was Nov. 13, 2010 against Montana State.
- The Lady Bears reached their first 12-0 start since the 2001-02 season, only the third time in Baylor history to do so.
- Baylor had won 50 of their last 54 games.
- Before tipoff Griner was presented with a ceremonial game ball marking her Big 12 record-breaking career blocks.

# BAYLOR 90 VS. MCNEESE STATE 50

Wednesday, Dec. 21, 2011, 7 p.m. CT
Ferrell Center, Waco
Attendance: 7,516

## LADY BEARS ROLL OVER ANOTHER SPEED BUMP

Returning to the Ferrell Center from their hard-fought win against No. 2 UConn the Lady Bears had a rough start against nonranked McNeese State in their last game before Christmas. Baylor handed the ball to the Cowgirls four times in the first two minutes and totaled 23 turnovers by the game's end.

"That was terrible. At half, we had too many turnovers," said Kim Mulkey. "But give credit to McNeese. They created those turnovers."

Named both Big 12 and National Player of the Week, Brittney Griner had 15 points, 13 rebounds and 4 blocks in just 24 minutes. Instead of playing aggressively to the rim she unselfishly passed to other players, and five other teammates scored in double figures. Freshman Sune Agbuke played a career high 20 minutes and had a double-double with 10 points and 15 rebounds for Baylor, another career high.

"All Sune needs is minutes," Mulkey said, acknowledging that Agbuke's floor time is limited because of other players. "She's caught in a numbers thing ... but I'm telling you the kid can flat-out play."

After a slow start the Lady Bears finished strong and gifted a 90-50 blowout to the Cowgirls.

# BAYLOR 93 VS. MISSISSIPPI VALLEY STATE 55

Wednesday, Dec. 30, 2011, 7 p.m. CT
Ferrell Center, Waco
Attendance: 7,634

## WRAPPING UP NONCONFERENCE PLAY

The Lady Bears returned to the court after Christmas break with a fiery performance. Baylor opened their last nonconference game with a 12-0 run and defeated Mississippi Valley State 93-55. The victory brought the Bears to a 13-0 season start for only the second time in the program's history.

Baylor led by 16 at the break and opened the second half with a 30-2 run during which seven Lady Bears scored. Five players had double figures: Brooklyn Pope (14), Odyssey Sims (11), Ashley Field (10), Destiny Williams (11), and Brittney Griner (20).

With the nonconference portion of their schedule complete, Coach Kim Mulkey focused on the challenge ahead.

"You can't be complacent after beating Notre Dame, Tennessee, and UConn. ... The Big 12 will humble you quickly. These next games will be more important than the nonconference games we have played. ... It's going to be brutal. We're going to have to work on blocking out and execution. We have got to execute better."

## STATS, STARS, AND STREAKS

- Baylor had prevented an opponent to shoot 50 percent in 187 straight games.
- Baylor had won 89 consecutive games scoring 70 or more points.
- Destiny Williams recorded a career high 14 rebounds and her fifth career double-double.
- Both women's (13-0) and men's (12-0) teams sported perfect records, the only Division I school to do so this season.

# LADY BEARS COACHING STAFF

## BILL BROCK
### ASSOCIATE HEAD COACH

During his nine seasons with Baylor, Associate Head Coach Bill Brock has played an instrumental role in forming the Lady Bears into a recognizable, renowned team. Brock serves as the team's recruiting coordinator in addition to working with Lady Bears post players and making defensive player assignments during games. His contributions have been crucial in making the Lady Bears' inside game one of the best in the nation. He has put together a number of stellar recruiting classes that have included All-Americans Sophia Young, Steffanie Blackmon, and Brittney Griner. Brock's coaching career began at Durant High School in Oklahoma, where he served as head boys' basketball coach from 1982 to 1985. Brock joined the Lady Bears program in 2000 and left briefly to coach the Lady Raiders at Texas Tech University. He returned to Baylor in 2009, much to the delight of the Lady Bears coaching staff.

## REKHA PATTERSON
### ASSISTANT COACH

Rekha Patterson began her career with the Lady Bears as a graduate assistant, moved up the ranks to become the coordinator of basketball operations, and is now in her first season as an assistant coach. In her current position Patterson assists with recruiting, manages the program's Nike account, and oversees the team's academics and community service activities in addition to providing instruction on the court. A graduate of North Carolina A&T State University, in 2004 she earned her master's degree in education from Baylor, with an emphasis on sports management. Patterson served as the teams' graduate assistant from 2002 to 2004, the period during which Baylor was the WNIT runner-up (2003) and advanced to the NCAA Tournament's Sweet 16 for the first time in school history (2004). Upon graduation from Baylor she made coaching stops at Creighton, Ball State, and Eastern Illinois before returning to the Lady Bears program.

## DAMION McKINNEY
### ASSISTANT COACH

Waco native Damion McKinney is in his sixth year as a member of the Lady Bears coaching staff. As an assistant coach McKinney works primarily with the Lady Bear guards and in recruiting. He has played an instrumental role in recruiting top talent to the Lady Bears program. His contributions include signing the nation's No. 1 recruiting class in 2009, transferring to Baylor two McDonald's All American players, and signing the top players in the state of Texas in 2008, 2009, and 2010. These players have gone on to win multiple honors, among them back-to-back National Freshman of the Year, Big 12 Freshman of the Year, and other Big 12 Conference awards. A graduate of Midwestern State University in Wichita Falls, Texas, McKinney came to Baylor's women's basketball program from the Dallas-based DFW Elite Basketball organization where he was the recruiting coordinator.

# LINDSAY PALMER
# #25

POSITION: Guard
CLASS: Senior
HEIGHT: 5' 11"
HOMETOWN: Tulsa, Okla.

Lindsay Palmer is most noted for her exceptional mastery of both academics and athletics. In 2012 Palmer was one of six Big 12 players to earn three-time Academic All-Big 12 honors for her top-rate academic performance during her time playing for the Lady Bears. This season she was one of only two Big 12 players to earn a 4.0 GPA.

Palmer completed her bachelor's degree in psychology within three years and graduated in May 2011. She is currently working toward a master's degree in public health and community health education and plans on working in the drug rehabilitation field.

Commended by her coaches as an easygoing, reliable player, Palmer established herself as a solid presence at game time as well as on the practice court, pushing her teammates toward excellence. In addition to her dedication to the Lady Bears and her studies, Palmer found time to serve others. For three consecutive summers she traveled to Kenya with a Baylor sports ministry team that hosted sports clinics in Nairobi and repaired a rehabilitation house.

# STATS, STARS, AND STREAKS

- The Lady Bears reached a season high with eight 3-pointers.
- Baylor is now 9-7 all-time in Big 12 Conference openers.
- With eight blocks Griner reached the 25th eight-plus block effort of her career and third this season.
- Jordan Madden registered a season high in points (12).
- Kimetria Hayden (14 points) tied a career high in assists (6).

# BAYLOR 90 VS. MISSOURI 46

Wednesday, Jan. 4, 2012, 7 p.m. CT
Ferrell Center, Waco
Attendance: 8,017

## MOVE OVER MIZZOU

The first Big 12 opener of the season for both Baylor and Missouri proved to be no contest for the Lady Bears. Baylor crushed the Tigers in a 90-46 conference win for the first 14-0 start in Lady Bear program history.

"It was very fun out there," said Jordan Madden. "Winning and getting a lot of steals and rebounds made the game so much more enjoyable." By the game's end Kim Mulkey had cleared her bench. Nine Baylor players added to the scoreboard, five of them in double digits. Odyssey Sims tallied 22 points while Brittney Griner made 14.

"You saw what we are capable of doing when two or three people are hanging on Griner," said Kim Mulkey. "The roles that everybody played tonight made us a very difficult team to beat. ... I've told Nae-Nae [Hayden] and Jordan [Madden] that they will decide if we make it to a Final Four and win a national championship. You know how they are going to guard Odyssey, you know what you're going to see with Brittney, but with Nae-Nae and Jordan, they have to accept the challenge to defend on the defensive end, make big shots, get steals and run the floor."

Missouri coach Robin Pingeton applauded the Bears' performance, "They're the elite, the best of the best."

# BAYLOR 57 VS. IOWA STATE 45

Saturday, Jan. 7, 2012, 7 p.m. CT
Hilton Coliseum, Ames, Iowa
Attendance: 9,103

## GRINER LEADS, IOWA FALLS

An aggressive Iowa State gave the Lady Bears a run for their money during the team's first Big 12 Conference road trip and second conference game.

Focused on the final goal, Kim Mulkey commented, "This is life on the road. This is just one of many. It prepares you. It prepares you for the playoffs."

Though it was not a cakewalk, Baylor protected their No. 1 ranking for another week and held on to their perfect season record. Brittney Griner—who scored only 10 points as a freshman in her first game against Iowa State two years ago—scored 26 points, her 10th time to score 20-plus points this season. Griner led the team in scoring with other Lady Bears players contributing 31 points to the team's final score. Jordan Madden made a total 11 points, 10 in the second half alone. Kimetria Hayden, tying a career high with 6 assists, had 8 points. Destiny Williams also added 8 points. Although she had been averaging 17.8 points, Odyssey Sims scored only two but had four steals and maintained pressure on Iowa offense.

Baylor's 57-45 win over Iowa State was a reversal of the outcome of the Bears' last trip to Ames in 2010 when the Cyclones posted a 69-45 victory.

# STATS, STARS, AND STREAKS

- The win made Baylor 153-89 in Big 12 regular season play and 126-52 under Mulkey.
- Baylor's 57 points were a season low after 66 vs. UConn.
- Baylor continued to be the only Division I school with both women's and men's teams achieving perfect records.
- Baylor leads the series against Iowa 13-6.

# ODYSSEY SIMS
## #0

POSITION: Guard
CLASS: Sophomore
HEIGHT: 5' 9"
HOMETOWN: Irving, Tex.

Odyssey Sims is widely recognized as Baylor women's basketball's rising star. As a sophomore she has already been nominated for various prestigious awards, including the John R. Wooden Award for outstanding collegiate basketball player and the Nancy Leiberman Award, which honors the nation's top collegiate point guard. One of the nation's best on-ball defenders, Sims was also named to the Midseason Naismith Trophy List. On March 23 Sims was recognized as a State Farm Wade Trophy finalist.

Sims is a standout player in the Big 12 Conference, ranked No. 5 in assists and free throw percentage. Honored with placement on the 2011-12 All-Big 12 first team, Sims was also named to the conference's All-Defensive team and to the seven-member Women's Basketball Coaches Association All-Region 5 team.

Among the nation's leaders in steals, Sims' remarkable performance this season tremendously contributed to the Lady Bears unparalleled winning season. Going into the NCAA tournament she averaged three steals per game. Ranked No. 7 for scoring among the Big 12 teams, Sims averaged 20.8 points per match against Baylor's nine ranked opponents this season.

Sims selected Baylor over schools such as Louisiana State University and Texas A&M because it was close to home. A speech communication major, she aspires to play professional basketball after graduation.

# BAYLOR 71 VS.
# OKLAHOMA STATE 44

Wednesday, Jan. 11, 2012, 7 p.m. CT
Ferrell Center, Waco
Attendance: 8,707

## STARRING GRINER AND SIMS

Back home in Waco the Lady Bears faced off against Oklahoma State in their third conference game of the regular season. Although they never trailed during the match, Baylor had a difficult time finding their rhythm during the first half and led only 26-24 at the break. Half of these points were scored by Brittney Griner. The Lady Bears returned to the court with a spark in their step and scored 20 points withinin the first seven minutes back on the floor.

National Player of the Year contender and All-America candidate Griner led the team in scoring with 28 points and 11 rebounds. Teammate and fellow All-America pick Odyssey Sims found her groove in the second half and hit a streak of triple three-pointers in a two-minute span, finishing with 21 points.

The game carried more than just a competitive air as Baylor fans and players recognized the sensitivity of the match for Oklahoma State. OSU's head and assistant women's basketball coaches were killed in a plane crash on Nov. 17 while on a recruiting trip in Arkansas. Fans were given orange ribbons to wear in memory of the coaches and greeted Cowgirls' coach Jim Littell with a standing ovation when he entered the court.

"The fans from Baylor are very classy and very knowledgeable and that was something that was much appreciated. I did notice it and I thought that was a sign of class," said Littell.

# STATS, STARS, AND STREAKS

- This was Baylor's fourth straight win over OSU.
- The Lady Bears reached a season high with 13 blocks.
- Griner moved to third place on Baylor's single-season blocks list with the eight she made during the game. She now holds the top three single-season totals in school history. This was the 26th time in her career to make at least eight blocks.
- Destiny Williams made her presence known with a double-double of 11 points and 13 rebounds.

# BAYLOR 77 VS. TEXAS 59

Sunday, Jan. 15, 2012, 1:30 p.m. CT
Frank Erwin Center, Austin, Tex.
Attendance: 9,002

## LONGHORNS GET THE HOOK

Baylor put the kibosh on the Longhorns four days after Texas conquered defending national champion Texas A&M in College Station. Going into the game Baylor was one of the two remaining undefeated teams in NCAA Division I programs; the Horizon League's Green Bay Phoenix also maintained a perfect record.

The Lady Bears' early 19-0 run laid the foundation for the win. At the half Baylor led by 20 (49-29) and Texas never could recover. Brittney Griner once again dominated the floor, tying her season high with 32 points. She made 21 of those before the break and, had she chosen to do so, could have approached and possibly surpassed her career-high 40 points. Unselfishly she passed to teammates. With 21 points Destiny Williams also tied her career high.

When Baylor reached a 30-point lead, Coach Kim Mulkey pulled players off the bench for time on the court. "I've just never been a coach to run up a score. I think you play as many players as you can, when you can, and we could today. I tried to get everybody on the floor."

The Lady Bears closed with an 18-point victory over the Longhorns in a final score of 77-59. Halfway through the season only two opponents, Tennessee and Connecticut, had come within 10 points of defeating Baylor.

## STATS, STARS, AND STREAKS

- The win brought the series against Texas to 23-57 total, 7-27 in Austin.

- Baylor continued its streak as the only Division I school with both women's and men's teams sporting perfect records (17-0 for both).

- Baylor held an opponent to under 50 percent shooting for 191 straight games.

- Kimetria Hayden recorded a career-high seven assists.

- Griner and Williams produced back-to-back double-doubles for the second time this season. They first accomplished the notable act vs. UCLA and Notre Dame and again against Oklahoma State and Texas.

SIC 'EM BEARS

# KIMETRIA "NAE-NAE" HAYDEN
# #1

**POSITION:** Guard
**CLASS:** Junior
**HEIGHT:** 6' 0"
**HOMETOWN:** Dallas. Tex.

Kimetria "Nae-Nae" Hayden stepped up her game during the latter part of the season and became a formidable presence on the hardwood. Hayden has been one of the team's top shooters this year, hitting .419 from the floor and averaging 9.3 points per game. Prior to the Sweet Sixteen match, Hayden had reached double-digit scoring for 15 games of the season and 28 of her career. During the Feb. 15 Oklahoma State contest, Hayden scored a season-high 20 points. Her accomplishments were recognized in March when she was named a 2011-12 All-Big 12 honorable mention selection.

An unselfish player, Hayden ranked No. 2 among the team in assists. The Baylor vs. Texas Tech game on Mar. 8 marked the 10th game this season in which Hayden delivered five or more assists. She delivered a career-high eight assists during the Big 12 Semifinals against Kansas State on Mar. 9.

Baylor's high academic and athletic standards, as well as the school's proximity to her Dallas home, appealed to Hayden, leading her to choose green and gold over Texas Tech, the University of Texas, and Oklahoma State. A junior health, human performance, and recreation major, Hayden aspires to play in the Women's National Basketball Association upon completing her collegiate basketball career.

# BAYLOR 72 VS. TEXAS TECH 64

Wednesday, Jan. 18, 2012, 7 p.m. CT
United Spirit Arena, Lubbock, Tex.
Attendance: 12,403

## TECH'S TOUGH TRY

No. 17 Texas Tech greeted their top-ranked guests with a challenging offense that forced Baylor to step up their defensive play. Yet despite their best efforts the Lady Raiders could not hold down the Lady Bears and succumbed to a 72-64 defeat.

Coach Kim Mulkey commented that her Lady Bears' defense "didn't look too pretty, but we won."

Texas Tech players closely guarded Baylor's reigning Big 12 Player of the Week, but Brittney Griner powered through and made 11 points and 4 rebounds in the first half. Baylor was up 37-31 at the half and pushed ahead after the break with a 10-0 run to advance their lead. Destiny Williams made her third straight double-double of the season with 16 points and a career-high 16 rebounds.

While the outcome of the matchup was desirable, Williams echoed the mantra of the season and put the victory in perspective. "We have a bigger goal and that's to win a national championship."

# STATS, STARS, AND STREAKS

- Baylor and Green Bay Phoenix were still the only two Division I women's teams sporting perfect records.
- Baylor had won 19 of its last 20 regular-season Big 12 games. The last loss, which broke Baylor's 21-game win streak, was at Texas Tech on Feb. 19, 2011.
- Baylor had won 92 consecutive games when scoring 70 or more points.
- Williams recorded double-figure rebounds by halftime in two straight games.
- With 21 points, Griner tallied double figures in 58 straight games and in 88 of 90 in her career. For the 13th time this season she notched 20-plus points.

# BAYLOR 76 VS. KANSAS STATE 41

Saturday, Jan. 21, 2012, 7 p.m. CT
Ferrell Center, Waco
Attendance: 9,380

## WELCOME BACK WASHINGTON

The Lady Bears ended a busy week—three games in a seven-day span—with a home match against No. 23 Kansas State Wildcats, their second straight ranked opponent and sixth of the season. Baylor once again outperformed their challenger 76-41 and notched their 19th win of the season.

But it was not the newly earned status of longest active winning streak in NCAA Division I women's basketball that the Lady Bears celebrated that evening. It was the return of redshirt sophomore Shanay Washington to the Ferrell Center for the first time since November 2010. Washington suffered an ACL tear during practice last season and underwent a follow-up surgery during the summer. She went 0-1 during the four minutes she played in the game against Texas Tech a few days prior. Washington contributed six points while playing only six minutes in her home court season debut.

Though it took them a few minutes to find their groove, the Lady Bears went on a 12-0 run early in the game and never slowed down. Kim Mulkey put in her remaining players at the eight-minute mark. The reserves maintained the momentum and scored a total 26 points to wrap up Baylor's sixth win against a Top 25 team.

"I liked everything about tonight," said Mulkey. "I'm so proud that everybody played, scored, and contributed something good. The proudest I am is of Shanay, just to see her back on that floor and playing well."

## STATS, STARS, AND STREAKS

- The Lady Bears shot above 41.7 percent in 18 of 19 games at this point in the season.
- Baylor reached a season high with a combined team total of 60 rebounds.
- This was the third time this season that all available Lady Bears recorded at least one point.
- With a career total of 520, Brittney Griner became the school's all-time leader in free throws made.

# JORDAN MADDEN
## #3

**POSITION:** Guard
**CLASS:** Junior
**HEIGHT:** 6' 0"
**HOMETOWN:** Lepanto, Ark.

Jordan Madden's impressive performance helped keep the Lady Bears at the top of their game throughout the 2011-12 season. Her double-digit scoring efforts contributed to the team's remarkable game score average of more than 70 points. She reached a season-high 12 points during the Missouri game on Jan. 4 and notched her sixth double-digit score of the season, 13th of her career, during the NCAA tournament game against Florida. Madden matched her season-high eight rebounds during the Baylor vs. Oklahoma State game on Feb. 15; she also made eight rebounds against Iowa State in January. Madden's career-high seven assists during Big 12 tournament play against Kansas State factored into the Lady Bears' conference championship win.

A junior health, human performance, and recreation major, Madden selected Baylor over a number of universities, including Texas A&M, Arkansas, and Mississippi, because of Baylor's high standards in both academics and athletics, and because of the excellence of the women's basketball program. Upon completing her basketball career, Madden aspires to become a basketball coach.

# BROOKLYN POPE
## #32

POSITION: Forward/Post
CLASS: Junior
HEIGHT: 6' 1"
HOMETOWN: Fort Worth, Tex.

A transfer from Rutgers University, Brooklyn Pope's noteworthy performance on the basketball court is a valuable addition to the Lady Bears. One of the team's top rebounders, Pope has played a pivotal role in helping the Lady Bears achieve a successful season. Her 13 points against Texas on Feb. 21 contributed to the memorable victory when the Lady Bears earned the Big 12 regular season championship. Pope kicked off the first NCAA tournament game with a great start, scoring 13 points—her 12th double-digit scoring game of the season—and seven rebounds against The University of California, Santa Barbara.

Pope is a junior health, human performance, and recreation major and admits that Baylor was where she always wanted to be. Her decision to attend Baylor was solidified by the coaching staff; she felt that Coach Kim Mulkey could help cultivate her athletic ability and make her a stronger player. Pope has many interests and hobbies, and in her spare time enjoys rapping.

- Six players scored in double digits for the first time since McNeese State, Dec. 21, 2011.
- Baylor hasn't allowed an opponent to shoot 50 percent in 194 straight games.
- Odyssey Sims and Terran Condrey scored 14 points apiece.
- Destiny Williams had 13 points, and Kimetria Hayden and Brooklyn Pope each had 10.

# BAYLOR 89 VS. OKLAHOMA 58

Thursday, Jan. 26, 2012, 7 p.m. CT
Lloyd Noble Center, Norman, Okla.
Attendance: 8,103

## PERFECT RECORD PERSISTS

Brittney Griner once again stumped the competition when the No. 1 Lady Bears traveled to Oklahoma to take on the Sooners in their home territory. Oklahoma spent the first half of the game steering clear of the shot-blocking tower and then reversed their strategy after the break to guard Griner forcefully. Griner's solid performance of 7 blocks and 18 points, including her first 3-pointer of the season, proved that neither Sooner approach was successful.

The Lady Bears led at the half by 15 points and pushed ahead of the Sooners even farther with a 12-0 run in the second period. Baylor's 31-point victory margin—the largest for Baylor in the 38-game series—paled against last year's match in Norman when the Lady Bears eked by with a one-point win. With such an advanced lead, Baylor's reserves hit the floor and contributed to the final 89 points. Six Lady Bears hit double figures.

"When you have six players in double figures and you have players like Terran [Condrey], who come off the bench, those players could be starters in many programs," said Kim Mulkey. "It gave us an opportunity to win on the road. I thought our defense was pretty special."

# BAYLOR 74 VS. KANSAS 46

Saturday, Jan. 28, 2012, 7 p.m. CT
Ferrell Center, Waco
Attendance: 10,006

## GRINER MOVES TO 2ND ON NCAA LIST

Back in Waco the Lady Bears felt right at home with family members in attendance cheering them on, inspiring energetic play that began at tipoff and lasted throughout the entire two periods. Baylor opened with a 14-4 run and never backed down, holding Big 12's No. 2 Kansas to 29 percent shooting and eventually crushing them 74-46. The Lady Bears paused during halftime to pay tribute to their personal pillars of support during Family Night.

With 28 points and 5 blocks, Baylor's junior center tour de force, Brittney Griner, pushed her way into second place on the NCAA list for career blocks with 506. Though despite her record-breaking performance this season, her job was still far from over.

"I said to [the team] after the game that they need to stay focused," said Coach Kim Mulkey. She also called on the fans to continue pushing them toward the goal. "Fans have to stay into it too. I look up and the fans are dead out there at the 10-minute mark. They were sitting in those seats, which I'm appreciative of, but we have got to stay focused. We can't become complacent. While we are so proud of our 21 wins, we still haven't won a championship."

## STATS, STARS, AND STREAKS

- Griner now only trails Saint Mary's star Louella Tomlinson, who had 663 career blocks.

- Griner scored 20-plus points for the 15th time this season.

- Destiny Williams (11 rebounds) registered double-digit rebounds in five of her last six games.

- Griner and Odyssey Sims were two of 20 national players named to the midseason Wooden Award list based on their performances in November, December, and January.

- The crowd of 10,006 was the fourth largest home crowd of the season.

# BAYLOR 71 VS. MISSOURI 41

Wednesday, Feb. 1, 2012, 7 p.m. CT
Mizzou Arena, Columbia, Mo.
Attendance: 3,504

## THE GRINER EFFECT STRIKES

Baylor's rematch against Missouri ended much like the first. The Tigers took their only lead early on at 4-2 but could not keep pace with the Lady Bears as the game progressed. Baylor led 28-18 at the half and left Mizzou in the dust after the break as the Lady Bears pulled away for a final score of 71-41.

Coach Kim Mulkey alerted her players before the game that their previous win against Mizzou should not be a factor with this game. "We can't look at the fact that we have played them already. It's 0-0; let's go play."

The Tigers anticipated the challenges of playing against star athlete Brittney Griner but still could not thwart the Griner Effect. With a final total of 18 points, Griner scored Baylor's first 8 points. The season's fourth-time Big 12 Player of the Week eventually found herself on the bench for much of the second half as the game grew ever more lopsided. Kimetria Hayden landed two 3-pointers for a total 15 points, her ninth double-digit scoring performance of the season. Odyssey Sims tallied 12 points to record her 17th double-digit game of the season.

# STATS, STARS, AND STREAKS

- This was the second time this season that Baylor held its opponents to no double-figure scorers. The first was against Howard, Nov. 11, 2011.

- Baylor hadn't allowed an opponent to shoot 50 percent in 196 straight games.

- Destiny Williams registered her sixth double-double (10 points, 11 rebounds) of the season and ninth of her career.

- Jordan Madden (2 blocks) recorded her third multiple-block game of the season.

# DESTINY WILLIAMS
## #10

POSITION: Forward/Post
CLASS: RS Junior
HEIGHT: 6' 1"
HOMETOWN: Benton Harbor, Mich.

Lady Bear Destiny Williams established herself early on as a formidable offensive force on the court and continued to elevate her game for the duration of the season. Averaging more than 10 points a game, Williams, along with Brittney Griner and Odyssey Sims, comprised the Baylor trio that led the team in double-digit scoring this season. Described by Kim Mulkey as a "quiet" and "tremendous" offensive player, Williams was one of the team's top rebounders, averaging nine rebounds per game. In Big 12 play Williams had double-doubles in 13 games. Her outstanding play carried over into the 2011-12 NCAA tournament; Georgia Tech's coach admitted that Williams' performance in the first 10 minutes of the Sweet Sixteen round forced the Yellow Jackets to adjust their defensive strategy for the game, and she finished the match with 18 points.

Williams' talent has garnered the attention of prestigious athletics associations. The Women's Basketball Coaches Association selected her along with teammates Griner and Sims for the seven-member State Farm Coaches' All-Region 5 team and also named her as a candidate for the 2012 WBCA Coaches' All-America Basketball Team. A transfer from the University of Illinois, Williams was also selected to the All-Big 12 Second Team and to the Big 12 Championship's All-Tournament team.

# MAKENZIE ROBERTSON
# #14

POSITION: Guard
CLASS: Sophmore
HEIGHT: 5' 10"
HOMETOWN: McGregor, Tex.

Sophomore Makenzie Robertson has brought a fresh set of talents to Baylor and to the Lady Bears program. The pre-business major is believed to be the only student athlete at Baylor to compete on two NCAA tournament teams in different sports—basketball and softball. Upon the conclusion of the 2011 Elite Eight game, Robertson joined Baylor's softball team, scoring 6 runs in 25 games and participating in the Women's College World Series.

Robertson, a central Texas native, has been an asset to the team both on and off the court. Robertson contributed to the Lady Bears' record-breaking season as a dependable reserve. She made a memorable shot in the Big 12 game against Kansas State when she netted an impressive 3-pointer with just 5:52 left in the game. The student athlete brought academic honors to the program by earning her first Academic All-Big 12 First Team recognition in February.

Though Robertson considered Southern Methodist University and Rice University, the daughter of Coach Kim Mulkey selected Baylor because of the opportunity to play on elite athletic teams and remain in an area close to her heart. A natural competitor, Robertson enjoys any kind of sport and desires to win a national championship while pushing herself to excel as a player.

# BAYLOR 70 VS. KANSAS STATE 41

Saturday, Feb. 4, 2012, 7 p.m. CT
Bramlage Coliseum, Manhattan, Kan.
Attendance: 12,528

## GRINER EXCEEDS 2,000 POINTS

Kansas State forced Baylor to step up their defense early in the game as the Lady Bears offense was unexpectedly off-kilter at the start. The Wildcats pushed for a 19-13 lead in the first half, but the buck stopped there. Baylor kicked it into high gear and smoked Kansas State by 29 points in front of a sellout crowd that had paid a dollar to see the contest.

Coach Kim Mulkey lectured on the importance of a dedicated fan base. "[Kansas State Coach Patterson] has a top-25 team out there. You should not have to sell $1 tickets to get them in the arena, not when you have the No. 1 team playing here. ... They do not just need to be here tonight, they need to be supporting their team every night."

With 29 points, Big 12's leading scorer Brittney Griner hit yet another milestone when she became the first player in Division I women's basketball to record 2,000 points and 500 blocked shots.

"I am glad she is on my team because I could not tell you how to guard her," Mulkey said of Griner.

# STATS, STARS, AND STREAKS

- Thus far Baylor had held 11 opponents under 30 percent shooting. Kansas State shot 26.4 percent and Baylor shot 56.3.
- Mulkey coached her 400th Baylor game.
- Griner's 29 points brought her career total to 2,020.
- Destiny Williams' 14 points marked her 12th double-figure score of the season and the 20th of her career.
- Odyssey Sims notched 13 points to record her 18th double-digit game of the season and 41st of her career.

# BAYLOR 81 VS. OKLAHOMA 54

Monday, Feb. 6, 2012, 8 p.m. CT
Ferrell Center, Waco
Attendance: 8,341

## A ROUGH ROUT

In an ESPN Big Monday/Rivalry Week game, the continually No. 1 ranked Lady Bears handed over another defeat to the Sooners only 11 days after beating them 89-58 in their home court in Norman. Both teams sported pink-hued jerseys in the designated Play 4Kay event to show support for breast cancer awareness.

Oklahoma tried to prevent Brittney Griner from her usual offensive feats in what Coach Kim Mulkey said was likely the roughest game of the season. Griner proved the Sooners' attempts were not effective by scoring 27 points, 13 of them free throws.

"It was a physical game, but it was a good game," Griner said. "I like games when you have to battle."

"There are times in practice where all we do is play defense, so it's nothing new to us," commented Brooklyn Pope, who netted 11 points. "Otherwise you're going to get pulled out. Do you want to play on national TV or watch on national TV? So we play defense."

After the win the ESPN commentator posed the question of the season, "Will anyone beat Baylor this year?" Only time would tell.

# STATS, STARS, AND STREAKS

- The Lady Bears have won four straight games over Oklahoma, though Oklahoma leads the series 24-15.
- Baylor's 13 blocked shots tie a season high. Baylor blocked 13 shots against Oklahoma State on Jan. 11, 2012.
- Griner set a career high with 13 made free throws.
- With seven assists Kimetria Hayden tied a career high that matched the seven she made against Texas on Jan. 15, 2012.
- Destiny Williams' 15 rebounds marked a season high and one away from a career high.

# BAYLOR 71 VS. TEXAS A&M 48

Saturday, Feb. 11, 2012, 5 p.m. CT
Ferrell Center, Waco
Attendance: 10,627

## AVENGING A LOSS & BIDDING FAREWELL

The Lady Bears faced off against Texas A&M in the Ferrell Center for what Coach Kim Mulkey deemed the last time, referring to A&M's less-than-amicable split from the Big 12 conference. Eleven months had passed since the Aggies sent Baylor back to Waco after defeating them in the Elite Eight round of the 2011 NCAA tournament. Motivated by the memory, Baylor dealt their longtime rival and the defending national champions a whopping 71-48 blow before a sellout crowd and national television audience.

"We didn't want a repeat of that game, so we came out strong and finished strong, too," said Brittney Griner.

The Lady Bears debuted new Nike Hyper Elite Platinum uniforms designated for wear by only two of the nation's top women's basketball teams in select games during the 2012 season. Each fan received a complimentary coordinating platinum t-shirt to wear during the match. The eventful evening commenced with the national anthem performance by country music star Trace Adkins. Despite the distractions of the night, Mulkey's team remained focused on the task at hand.

"Other than the win, what I was most proud of was that our team was able to compartmentalize all of it," said Mulkey. "A lot of things could have distracted us, but it was all good and I thought our team did their part to make it a great day."

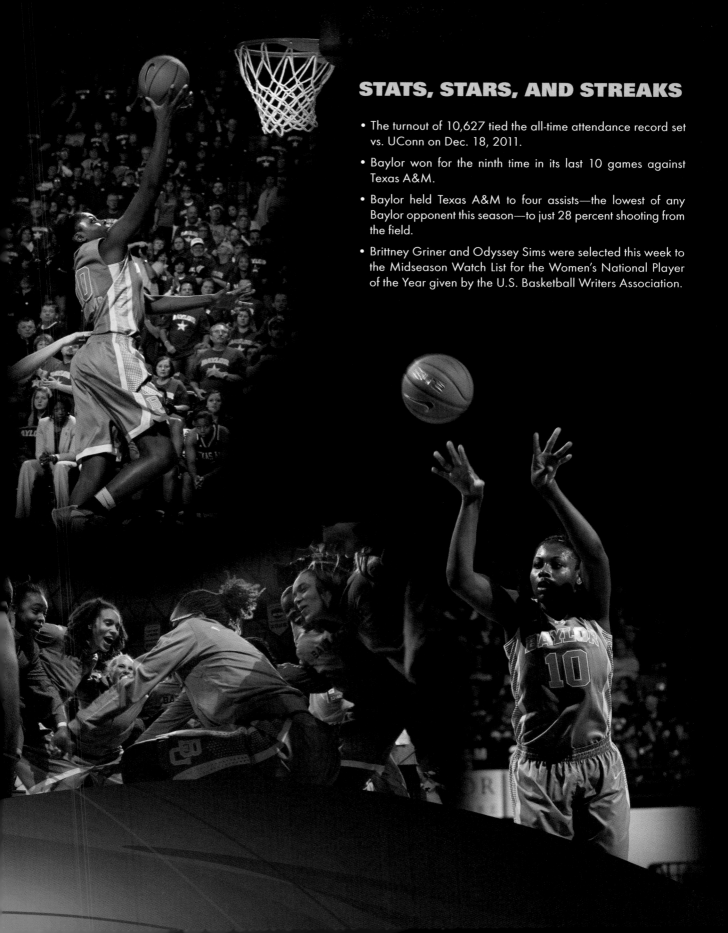

## STATS, STARS, AND STREAKS

- The turnout of 10,627 tied the all-time attendance record set vs. UConn on Dec. 18, 2011.

- Baylor won for the ninth time in its last 10 games against Texas A&M.

- Baylor held Texas A&M to four assists—the lowest of any Baylor opponent this season—to just 28 percent shooting from the field.

- Brittney Griner and Odyssey Sims were selected this week to the Midseason Watch List for the Women's National Player of the Year given by the U.S. Basketball Writers Association.

# BAYLOR 83 VS. OKLAHOMA STATE 52

Wednesday, Feb. 15 2012, 7 p.m. CT
Gallagher–IBA Arena, Stillwater, Okla.
Attendance: 2,648

## THE STREAK CONTINUES

The tornadic Lady Bears stormed into Stillwater and swept away the Cowgirls with yet another win, extending Baylor's perfect season record to 26-0. Oklahoma State may have thought they had a winning chance with an early two-point lead, but Brittney Griner and her squad squelched those hopes with a 17-point lead at the half that turned into a 83-52 victory for Baylor.

Kimetria Hayden scored a season-high 20 points becoming the third Lady Bear to score at least 20 points in a match this season. Griner had 28 points, her 19th time this season to score over 20 points. After halftime the reserves began to trickle in, and by the game's end every Lady Bear had minutes on the floor.

The week was packed with multiple honorable announcements for Baylor. USA Basketball named Griner along with former Lady Bear and current WNBA standout Sophia Young as two of 21 finalists for the 2012 U.S. Olympic Women's Basketball Team. Griner was the only collegiate player on the list. Only days prior Griner had been recognized as Phillips Big 12 Women's Basketball Player of the Week for the fifth time this season. Three members of the team, Lindsay Palmer, Ashley Field, and Makenzie Robertson, earned Academic All-Big 12 first-team honors. Palmer was one of just two Big 12 players to earn a 4.0 GPA.

## STATS, STARS, AND STREAKS

- Baylor's first 13-0 conference start in the Big 12 era surpassed last year's 11-0 start.

- The Lady Bears won the previous eight games by at least 20 points.

- Baylor had a shooting percentage of 54 and held the Cowgirls to 26 percent. The Lady Bears led the nation's average with 48.7.

- Jordan Madden tied her season-high in rebounds with eight.

# SHANAY WASHINGTON #4

POSITION: Guard
CLASS: RS Sophomore
HEIGHT: 6' 1"
HOMETOWN: Austin, Tex.

Sophomore Shanay Washington is the definition of perseverance. As a freshman, Washington started 32 of 36 games before suffering a tear to her left anterior cruciate ligament (ACL) in November 2010, which benched her for the remainder of the 2010-11 season. A follow-up surgery in July 2011 forced her to sit out the beginning of this season. She made her long-awaited debut against Texas Tech on Jan. 18, 2012 and appeared in 10 games before succumbing to yet another ACL tear in the same knee during the Feb. 21 Big 12 conference championship game against Texas. Even though her playing time this season was limited, she added 20 points to the team's undefeated record, even managing to throw in a pair of blocks against Oklahoma on Feb. 7 before her unfortunate return to the bench.

A general studies major, Washington passed up the University of Texas and Texas A&M for the opportunity to be part of Baylor's family-like atmosphere. Coach Kim Mulkey noted that the familial qualities of the team will be a necessary healing factor. "The best medicine for Shanay is going to be her teammates. They are the ones that are going to have to help her, and they will."

# BAYLOR 56 VS. TEXAS TECH 51

Saturday, Feb. 18, 2012, 7 p.m. CT
Ferrell Center, Waco
Attendance: 10,381

## BIG 12 TITLE IN REACH

Texas Tech demanded a rigorous rematch against the Lady Bears after losing by eight points on their home court in Lubbock exactly one month prior. Baylor's 56-51 win over the Lady Raiders ensured the Lady Bears at least a share of the Big 12 regular season championship. One more Big 12 win would set in stone a back-to-back title for the only undefeated team—men's or women's—in NCAA Division I.

The Lady Raiders led 35-30 by halftime, but Baylor changed their momentum after the break to fight for the win. A crucial tie-breaking layup by Destiny Williams in the second half pushed Baylor into the lead for the rest of the game. Tech's defense double and triple-teamed Brittney Griner throughout the night, though Griner still managed 18 points, 14 rebounds, and 6 blocks.

Upon the game's conclusion, the team was presented with their 2011 Big 12 championship trophy as a stand-in for the 2012 award. But the confetti-strewn celebration did not distract from the ultimate goal yet to be attained.

"Tonight's game definitely shows us that the rest of the games are not going to get any easier," said Griner. "A good game like this definitely helps get us prepared for the tournament because every game is going to be close."

"It's a good sign when you win, but even tonight if we had lost the game, you need environments like this to prepare you," commented Kim Mulkey.

## STATS, STARS, AND STREAKS

- This game was the third advance sell-out and had the third largest crowd this season.

- Baylor trailed at halftime for only the fourth time this season and first time in Big 12 play.

- Griner registered her fourth consecutive game with at least six blocks, and 56th career game with five-plus.

- With 16 points, Williams recorded her 13th double-figure scoring game of the season and 21st of her career.

# BAYLOR 80 VS.
# TEXAS 59

Tuesday, Feb. 21, 2012, 6:30 p.m. CT
Ferrell Center, Waco
Attendance: 8,592

## ONE TITLE DOWN, TWO MORE TO GO

The Big 12 regular season title officially belonged to the top-ranked Lady Bears for the second year in a row after they delivered a second blow to the University of Texas. The Longhorns found themselves outrebounded, outblocked, and outplayed by game's end with a 21-point loss.

The season's sixth-time Big 12 Player of the Week, the un-blockable Brittney Griner, scored her 40th career double-double in only 28 minutes in her 100th collegiate game. Griner was recognized in a pregame ceremony for becoming the fourth Lady Bear to score 2,000-points in her collegiate career. Earlier in the week standout Odyssey Sims received a nomination for the Lieberman Award recognizing the nation's top collegiate point guard in women's Division I basketball.

Misfortune struck with less than a minute remaining when Shanay Washington fell to the floor, suffering from a torn ACL in her left knee that had just recently healed. Washington appeared in 10 games this season after her debut against Texas Tech on Jan. 18.

With the team's third all-time Big 12 regular season championship in the bag, Kim Mulkey looked ahead to the remaining games of the season. "We're playing to win. That's what competitors do. You've got to play to win."

# STATS, STARS, AND STREAKS

- Baylor outrebounded Texas 51-39.
- Kimetria Hayden (17 points) registered her 13th double-figure scoring game of the season and 25th of her career.
- Odyssey Sims (6 assists) recorded her 10th game of the season with at least six assists.
- Brooklyn Pope (13 points) registered her 10th double-figure scoring game of the season and 18th of her career.
- Destiny Williams (11 points) notched her 14th double-figure scoring game of the season and 22nd of her career.
- The last home loss for the Lady Bears was in March 2009 against Texas. This win extended the school-record home win streak to 39.

# SUNE AGBUKE
## #22

POSITION: Post
CLASS: Freshman
HEIGHT: 6' 4"
HOMETOWN: San Antonio, Tex.

Freshman Sune Agbuke is a welcome addition to the Lady Bears basketball program. In her first season Agbuke has established herself as a force on the court.

She commenced her collegiate career with an impressive start, scoring 10 points and 15 rebounds, her first double-double, during the Baylor vs. McNeese State game on Dec. 21. Agbuke scored a season-high 11 points in the first round of the NCAA Championship against the University of California-Santa Barbara. Going into the Final Four match, the philosophy/pre-law major had notched 73 points during her first year as a Lady Bear.

Recruited by the Lady Bears program in 2010, she selected Baylor over schools such as the University of Oklahoma in Tulsa and the University of Miami because of what she describes as Baylor's "complete package": strong academics, a great athletics program, and a campus close to home. In addition to her notable athleticism, Agbuke has a hunger for knowledge and aspires to be a lawyer.

# BAYLOR 76 VS. KANSAS 45

Friday, Feb. 24, 2012, 6:30 p.m. CT
Allen Fieldhouse, Lawrence, Kan.
Attendance: 4,676

## THE GRINER EFFECT STRIKES AGAIN

The Lady Bears took their game on the road to Kansas and continued their undefeated streak with a 76-45 blowout against the Jayhawks. Kansas fell prey to the Griner Effect and struggled offensively, shooting just 26.9 percent from the field.

The Baylor win was collaborative with four players scoring in double figures and the entire team finding time on the hardwood. Nine Lady Bears played at least 10 minutes each as Coach Kim Mulkey rotated her crew to keep the starters rested and the reserves in shape for postseason play.

At 29-0 Baylor only needed to defeat Texas A&M in their next matchup to tie Nebraska for best season start in Big 12 history. Mulkey reiterated that an undefeated season was not Baylor's objective.

"That hasn't been a goal of ours; it's not on the goal board. ... It's the last six games we're focusing on and those are the last six games of the NCAA tournament."

## STATS, STARS, AND STREAKS

- Baylor extended its school-record Big 12 regular-season win streak to 19.

- Brittney Griner (20 points) has scored in double figures fo 99 of 101 games in her career.

- Kimetria Hayden (16 points) scored in double figures in fou of the last five games.

- Brooklyn Pope (10 points) scored in double figures for he 11th game this season.

- Odyssey Sims (15 points) recorded her 21st game of the sea son in double-digit scoring.

# BAYLOR 69 VS. TEXAS A&M 62

Monday, Feb. 27, 2012, 6 p.m. CT
Reed Arena, College Station, Tex.
Attendance: 10,265

## A CONQUEST IN COLLEGE STATION

The Lady Bears were greeted with tough competition and jeering fans during their last trip to College Station. Not pleased with their 71-48 loss in Waco, the No. 17 Aggies had prepared for the rematch, the last regular-season contest between the two rivals before Texas A&M's move to the Southeastern Conference next season.

Brittney Griner and Odyssey Sims scored 25 points each and both found themselves in foul trouble throughout the evening. With Griner on the bench for long stretches during both halves, the Aggies took advantage of her absence and stepped up their play, keeping the score close. Coach Kim Mulkey welcomed the challenge and used the situation to practice tough decision-making which they would likely encounter during the NCAA tournament.

A pivotal moment in the game occurred with three minutes remaining when Baylor led by three points and a likely out-of-bounds-destined ball bounced off an official to remain in play. Sims snatched up the ball for a layup and Kimetria Hayden followed with a jumper, bringing the score to 67-60 and ultimately sealing the win.

The ESPN2-televised victory pushed Baylor's undefeated season record to 30-0, equaling the 2009-10 Nebraska squad for the best start in Big 12 conference history.

## STATS, STARS, AND STREAKS

- This was Baylor's fourth straight victory against Texas A&M in College Station and moved Baylor to 49-36 all-time versus the Aggies.

- Baylor had not permitted an opponent to shoot 50 percent in 205 straight games.

- Odyssey Sims scored a season-high-tying 25 points and recorded the seventh 20-point game of the season, 14th of her career.

- Destiny Williams (12 rebounds) recorded her 14th double-digit rebounding game of the season, 18th of her career.

# LADY BEARS COACHING STAFF (CONTINUED)

## JOHNNY DERRICK
DIRECTOR OF BASKETBALL OPERATIONS

Johnny Derrick has served on the Lady Bears coaching staff for 12 years. He joined the Lady Bears program as an assistant coach in 2000, a position he held for seven seasons, during which Baylor won the 2005 Big 12 and NCAA Championship titles. Now in his fifth season as the team's director of basketball operations, the Dubach, La., native handles the business side of the program, including opponent scheduling, team travel coordination, and budget management.

## EDSEL HAMILTON IV
COORDINATOR OF BASKETBALL OPERATIONS

Edsel Hamilton has been with the Lady Bears basketball program for five years, this being his first as the coordinator of basketball operations. Prior to his current position, Hamilton spent two years as a graduate assistant with the team and two years as the program's first director of video operations. The Pflugerville, Texas, native manages the film exchange program, assists with recruit correspondence as well as opponent preparation, and coordinates the Lady Bear ball girls.

## CHERRISH WALLACE
STUDENT ASSISTANT

A junior from Pasadena, Calif., Cherrish Wallace served in her first season as a student assistant for the Lady Bears. Wallace initially played on the team for two seasons before medically retiring from basketball due to a chronic leg injury.

## MARIAH CHANDLER
## #44

POSITION: Post/Forward
CLASS: Junior
HEIGHT: 6' 2"
HOMETOWN: Atlanta, Ga.

Mariah Chandler, nicknamed "Miracle," is a passionate player and valuable ambassador for the Lady Bears. Although she was red-shirted this season, Chandler still contributed from the sidelines, boosting the team's morale and cheering them on to victory after victory. As a sophomore returning from knee surgery last season, Chandler played in 19 of 37 games, contributing 27 points.

Her enthusiasm for basketball and desire to serve others attracted her to join Baylor's sports ministry team, which traveled to Kenya in the summer of 2010. Chandler accompanied fellow teammates Melissa Jones and Lindsay Palmer, along with 27 other students, in hosting sports clinics and making repairs to a rehabilitation house in Nairobi.

Though she was pursued by Georgia Tech, Maryland, Florida State, Florida, and Texas, the film and digital media major chose Baylor because of the school's academic reputation and the women's basketball team's

# BAYLOR 77 VS. IOWA STATE 53

Saturday, Mar. 3, 2012, 11 a.m. CT
Ferrell Center, Waco
Attendance: 9,435

## AN UNDEFEATED REGULAR SEASON

The continuously top-ranked Lady Bears completed their first undefeated regular season in school history when they took down Iowa State 77-53 on their home court. The Cyclones started strong but could not keep up with their opponent when Baylor turned on full-court pressure defense and changed the pace of the game to become the Big 12 Conference's first 18-game winner.

Destiny Williams, one of the team's top-rebounders who collected her 15th double-digit rebounding game of the season with 11 makes during the match, reflected on the team's accomplishment of remaining undefeated: "It's an honor, but it really doesn't mean anything until you win a national championship."

The game capped off a week of honors for the Lady Bears. Baylor's three seniors, Terran Condrey, Ashley Field, and Lindsay Palmer, were recognized at halftime. Teammates Brittney Griner and Odyssey Sims joined 30 other top national players to be nominated for the Naismith Women's College Player of the Year Award. Griner, who led the Big 12 averaging 22.7 points per game going into the match, scored a career-high 41 points.

"We're pretty appreciative of it," National Coach of the Year nominee Kim Mulkey said of her team's feat. "It's on the backburner now. We're going to try to win three games in the Big 12 tournament, but we're focusing on those last six."

## STATS, STARS, AND STREAKS

- Baylor completed a school record 31-0 overall and 18-0 in league play.

- Throughout the season the team has won by an average margin of nearly 28 points.

- This win extended their home-court winning streak to 40 in a row.

- Griner passed her previous career high of 40 points against Green Bay in the NCAA Tournament last season.

# BIG 12 CHAMPIONSHIP
# QUARTERFINALS

## BAYLOR 72 VS. TEXAS TECH 48

Thursday, March 8, 2012, 1:30 p.m. CT
Municipal Auditorium, Kansas City, Mo.
Attendance: 5,542

### AND THE WINS KEEP COMING

Baylor's domination streak continued in the Phillips 66 Big 12 Conference tournament with a 72-48 win over Texas Tech in the quarterfinals, bringing Baylor's record to 32-0. The Lady Raiders set up a tough defense at the start and forced Baylor to adjust their play. The Lady Bears responded by turning on the full-court defense, creating a 24-point lead at the break and leaving Tech in the dust after the half. The win advanced Baylor to the semifinal round to take on No. 5 seed Kansas State.

"I thought we were very aggressive," Big 12 Coach of the Year Kim Mulkey said. "I thought we picked up too many fouls and had to sit players. At the same time, those players going to the bench gave other players opportunities." Every Lady Bear who hit the hardwood during the game scored.

"It was great. This program is way more than me," commented Brittney Griner, who was named Big 12 Player of the Year for the second straight season earlier in the week. "You can stop me, but you've got to stop everybody else on our team too. I love being able to sit on the bench and just watch my team play and execute and keep playing."

## STATS, STARS, AND STREAKS

- Griner was also named Big 12 Player of the Week for the seventh time this season and Big 12 Defensive Player of the Year for the third consecutive year.

- Odyssey Sims and Griner were both named to the All-Big-12 First Team and to the All-Defensive Team. They were also among 15 finalists named for the John R. Wooden Award.

- Destiny Williams was named to the All-Big-12 Second Team.

- Kimetria Hayden was an All-Big-12 Honorable Mention selection.

# BIG 12 CHAMPIONSHIP
# SEMIFINALS

## BAYLOR 86 VS. KANSAS STATE 65

Friday, March 9, 2012, 12 p.m. CT
Municipal Auditorium, Kansas City, Mo.
Attendance: 5,408

### GRINER BREAKS BIG 12 RECORD

The Lady Bears blew past No. 5 seed Kansas State 86-65 in the semifinals round of the Big 12 tournament, but the continuation of the Lady Bears' undefeated status was merely part of the game's complete story. Conference Player of the Year Brittney Griner played the best game of her collegiate career, setting a Big 12 tournament record with 45 points and shattering her previous career-high 41 points made during the regular season finale against Iowa State.

"I'm happy I got it," Griner said. "It would have been sweeter if it was 45 blocks." Griner also had 10 rebounds and seven blocks.

Baylor offense unselfishly kept passing to Griner, shelling out 26 assists led by Kimetria Hayden with eight and Jordan Madden with seven.

"The guards did a great job of passing her the ball, and she did a great job finishing," Destiny Williams said of Griner and of Baylor's teamwork. Williams made a stunning 14 rebounds and contributed a total 12 points to the game, as well.

Baylor advanced to the Big 12 Championship finals for the sixth time in program history.

## STATS, STARS, AND STREAKS

- Griner reached 2,278 points in her college career, moving her to No. 5 on the Big 12 career scoring chart.
- Destiny Williams recorded double-digit rebounds in a team-high 15 games this season, 20 in her career.
- Kimetria Hayden registered a career-high eight assists.
- Jordan Madden matched her career high with seven assists.

# PHILLIPS 66 BIG 12
# CONFERENCE CHAMPIONSHIP

## BAYLOR 73 VS. TEXAS A&M 50

Saturday, March 10, 2012, 11 a.m. CT
Municipal Auditorium, Kansas City, Mo.
Attendance: 4,235

### BACK-TO-BACK
### LADY BEARS CLAIM BIG 12 TOURNEY TITLE

*By Krista Pirtle*
*The Lariat*

Tying a program high 34 wins, the No. 1 Baylor Lady Bears can now check their second goal off the bucket list: Big 12 Tournament Champions.

Baylor defeated Texas A&M soundly 73-50 in what could be the final matchup for the foreseeable future.

The 23-point winning margin is the largest in Big-12 Championship title games.

Junior Destiny Williams and sophomore Odyssey Sims were named to the All-Tournament team, and junior Brittney Griner was named Most Outstanding Player for the second straight year.

Griner did not have many points, but she didn't need to. Odyssey Sims led the way with a season high 26 points.

"Coach just told me to attack," Sims said. "We ran our play. It was the high screen. Made it come off, made something happen. I had to either go to the rim or kick it out. And I just kept going until they tried to stop me."

She was followed by Williams, Griner and junior Jordan Madden with 12, 11 and 10 respectively.

"It's not Brittney Griner and Baylor," Griner said. "This is Baylor. We are a team. Everybody pulls together and contributes. I mean, I love games like this, watching my teammates score, and if I catch it, get double-teamed, kick it to them. And I love it. This is a special team and I love my team."

Williams also grabbed 11 boards for a double-double.

"If you look at what Destiny does around Brittney and through Brittney, she never stops what she's been asked to do: rebound the ball, score, put back, shoot the jumper at the foul line," Baylor head coach Kim Mulkey said. "Destiny has done that whether Griner gets four or 10 today."

The three point line did not impact the game much at all, with A&M hitting a pair and Baylor sinking only one.

Defensively Griner denied six shots, and Odyssey Sims snatched four steals.

Baylor began the game on a 10-0 run before the Aggies scored with 14:24 left in the first half. From then on, Texas A&M played the Lady Bears 18-18, but Baylor was up by 15 at the half and didn't let up.

*Continued on next page...*

"If we would have hit out bunnies and got it down to a nine or 10 point game I think our confidence-the first five minutes of the second half was all Baylor," Texas A&M head coach Gary Blair said. "And you give them the credit. They're a great basketball team. Baylor University has had a great year."

Twenty points came from the charity stripe for Baylor, thanks to entering the bonus with 15:06 to play.

Baylor shot 49 percent from the floor while holding Texas A&M to 27.9 percent on the afternoon.

From the paint Baylor did not have quite the advantage it had in previous games this tournament, only outscoring the Aggies 38-24.

"Well, it's exciting to win," Sims said. "We've been winning all season. We've been successful. But this is great. But now we're focused on six games. That's what we're striving for, and I'm saying we are having fun, but six games is the most important."

Now the team will focus on perfection with six games standing between it and the title of National Champions.

"I've really loved their mindset," Mulkey said. "They're not in that locker room high-fiving, oohing and ahhing, going crazy in there. It is more like a business approach. We took care of business here. Let's go to the men's game tonight, cheer hard, get on the plane, rest tomorrow, go to pairings Monday, and let's get ready for what you ultimately want, and that's the national championship."

*Student journalist Krista Pirtle's article originally appeared in The Lariat. Pirtle filed reports about the top-ranked Baylor Lady Bears throughout the season for The New York Times college sports blog The Quad.*

## BAYLOR 81 VS. UCSB 40

Sunday, Mar. 18, 2012, 1:45 p.m. CT
The Stroh Center, Bowling Green, Ohio
Attendance: 4,205

### GETTING DOWN TO BUSINESS

After a momentous Big 12 Championship victory, Baylor headed to Ohio to commence an undaunted march to their final destination, the NCAA championship finals in Denver. Assigned the No. 1 seed in the Des Moines region, the Lady Bears kicked off tournament play with high energy and notched an 81-40 win over UC-Santa Barbara to advance to the second round.

Baylor set the pace from the start, scoring the first 12 points of the games. Brittney Griner played her game as usual, blocking 2 shots and netting 14 points in just 22 minutes. Eleven Lady Bears played at least 12 minutes on the hardwood and demonstrated that teamwork was their greatest asset. Brooklyn Pope, Destiny Williams, Odyssey Sims, and Sune Agbuke all scored in double digits while Lindsay Palmer finished the game with an impressive 3-point shot.

"Lindsay's three was amazing," commented Griner. "We were very excited, but it's good to see [the reserves] out there ... we both get better and it shows."

The Lady Bears' defense proved too much for the Gauchos to handle, and 16th-seeded UCSB became the first victim of Baylor's quest to complete their unfinished business.

## STATS, STARS, AND STREAKS

- The win brought the Lady Bears' record to 35-0, the best in program history, surpassing last season's 34 wins.

- The Lady Bears claimed the highest active winning streak and remained the only undefeated team in NCAA Division I women's basketball.

- Baylor advanced to the NCAA Championship second round for the 10th time in program history.

- The win marked the 109th straight game scoring 70 or more points and the 92nd straight game with more than 80 points.

- Sune Agbuke tallied a career-high 11 points. Her previous high was 10 vs. McNeese State.

# NCAA CHAMPIONSHIP
# SECOND ROUND

## BAYLOR 76 VS. FLORIDA 57

Tuesday, Mar. 20, 2012, 6:05 p.m. CT
The Stroh Center, Bowling Green, Ohio
Attendance: 4,097

### A SLAM DUNK OF A WIN

Victory tasted sweet to Baylor as they felled yet another competitor standing in the way of the championship title. Ninth-seeded Florida fought hard, but the Lady Bears delivered a 76-57 defeat to disappointed Gator fans.

Not a team to surrender without a fight, Florida did their best to guard Baylor's star post Brittney Griner and prevent her from touching the ball. But Gator defense was no match for the 6-foot-8 tower who brought the game to a climax and the crowd to their feet when she slammed her first dunk of the season. After receiving a pass from teammate Kimetria Hayden, Griner made her epic drop-step, right-handed throwdown, becoming just the second woman to dunk during an NCAA tournament.

"That wasn't just a barely-over-the-rim type of dunk," Kim Mulkey said of Griner. "That was a monster dunk."

"I think my team got fired up a little bit more than me," said a modest Griner. "I got a little bit more fired up, I think, on one of the blocks I had. But it definitely felt good throwing it down."

In the end, Baylor triumphed for a solid win, remaining undefeated and advancing to the Sweet Sixteen round of competition.

## STATS, STARS, AND STREAKS

- Odyssey Sims (14 points), Jordan Madden (13 points), Destiny Williams (11 points), Kimetria Hayden (11 points), and Brittney Griner (25 points) all notched double-digit scores.

- Griner made a total of six blocks, increasing her NCAA Championship career block record to 71.

- This is Baylor's fourth straight year advancing to the NCAA Championship Sweet Sixteen and the seventh in program history.

- Griner is only the second woman to dunk in NCAA tournament history. Candace Parker of Tennessee holds the record for two dunks in an NCAA tournament game in 2006 against Army.

## BAYLOR 83 VS. GEORGIA TECH 68

Saturday, Mar. 24, 2012, 1:30 p.m. CT
Wells Fargo Arena, Des Moines, Iowa
Attendance: 7,941

### SWEET 16 A SLAM DUNK

Baylor progressed one step closer to completing unfinished business this season when they wiped out Georgia Tech in Sweet Sixteen competition in Des Moines, Iowa. All-American Brittney Griner rounded out an extraordinary performance with a two-handed dunk in the second half that brought the crowd to their feet and tied the record for most dunks in NCAA tournament play.

It was a shaky start for the Lady Bears against the Yellow Jackets' winningest team in school history, but after an early Baylor time-out the team turned up the heat with a 20-0 run and stayed on fire until the end. Griner tallied 35 points, 10 rebounds, and 6 blocks in addition to the dunk, the seventh slam of her career and her second straight game to perform the feat. Destiny Williams, whom Georgia Tech Coach MaChelle Joseph considered "a huge factor in the game," added 18 points. Coach Kim Mulkey attributed much of Baylor's success to her team's ability to handle Georgia Tech's press.

"I thought the difference in the game was Odyssey Sims, Nae-Nae Hayden, Jordan Madden, and Destiny Williams," Mulkey said. "Brittney got 35 points because of their ability to handle pressure and score at the end of the press."

Baylor's 83-68 victory over Georgia Tech advanced the Lady Bears to the Elite Eight round of the NCAA Championship for the third straight year and the fourth time in program history.

Mulkey assured the public that her approach to the forthcoming game against Tennessee would be the same as all the rest. "We're 37 games into it now. Our pressure come Monday won't be any different than it has been over the last 37 ball games."

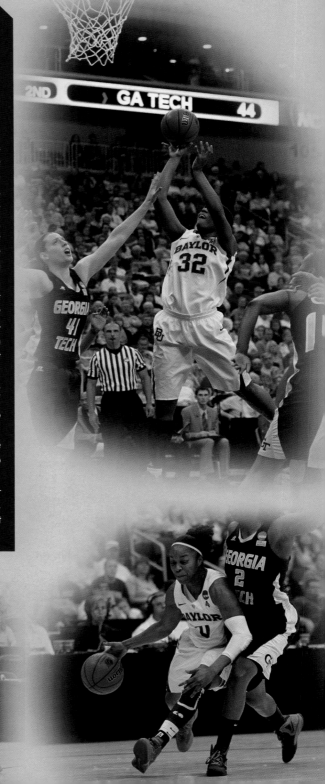

## STATS, STARS, AND STREAKS

- Baylor is the fifth team in the NCAA era to reach 37 wins in a single season.

- Members of Baylor's senior class—Terran Condrey, Ashley Field, and Lindsay Palmer—are 128-19 (.870) in their four years at Baylor.

- With her six game blocks, Griner extended her NCAA Championship career block record to 77. She scored 30 or more points for the fourth time this season and the 10th time in her career."

- Odyssey Sims scored 11 points and Brooklyn Pope contributed 9 points.

## BAYLOR 77 VS. TENNESSEE 58

Monday, Mar. 26, 2012, 6 p.m. CT
Wells Fargo Arena, Des Moines, Iowa
Attendance: 9,068

### ON TO THE FINAL FOUR

Baylor's prospects for a perfect season looked ever more promising after the Lady Bears raked in a celebrated Elite Eight win against Pat Summitt's second-seeded Tennessee squad. Each team had high stakes riding on the outcome: for the Lady Vols, a championship win for Coach Summitt in what was likely the last tournament of her career; for their seniors, the continuance of a longstanding Tennessee streak that each four-year class make a Final Four appearance; and for the Lady Bears, the completion of a championship-bound journey that commenced a season prior.

Baylor struggled offensively at the start, missing their first five shot attempts. Then Odyssey Sims took charge and set the tone on both offensive and defensive ends of the court. She and teammate Kimetria Hayden kept the rim hot throughout the match, with Sims netting 27 points and Hayden tallying 18, with 13 of those in the first half. Brittney Griner finished the game one block shy of a triple-double with 23 points, 15 rebounds, and 9 blocks.

The game hit a snag when Griner, Terran Condrey, and Jordan Madden were ejected with less than a minute remaining. The three Lady Bears left the bench to break up a small skirmish that ensued between Sims and Tennessee's Shekinna Stricklen after Sims tumbled to the floor. The scuffle did not get physical and no players were suspended, but Stricklen and Sims each received a technical foul for unsportsmanlike conduct.

Destiny Williams summed up the team's sentiment about advancing to the Final Four: "We're so happy, but you can't relax. We have two more games left and now we have to prepare and continue to play so we can finish it as a champion."

# STATS, STARS, AND STREAKS

- Baylor advanced to the Final Four for the second time in three years and the third time overall.
- The win brought the Lady Bears' season record to 38-0.
- Brittney Griner was named the outstanding player in the Des Moines Regional, and Odyssey Sims and Destiny Williams were named to the Des Moines Regional's All-Tournament team.
- Griner and Sims were selected as State Farm Wade Trophy Finalists.

# NCAA CHAMPIONSHIP
# FINAL FOUR

## BAYLOR 59 VS. STANFORD 47

Sunday, Apr. 1, 2012, 8 p.m. CT
The Pepsi Center, Denver, Colo.
Attendance: 19,028

### FIVE GAMES DOWN, ONE TO GO

The remaining four teams competed on Sunday, Apr. 1, for the chance to move on to the NCAA finals. Notre Dame knocked out Connecticut in the first contest of the evening after an intense overtime period. Then it was time for top-ranked Baylor and No. 2 Stanford to step onto the court and battle for the coveted last spot in the final championship round.

Stanford did their homework to prepare for the Griner Effect and worked up a unique strategy in an effort to block the Lady Bears from their 40-0 destination. Cardinal offense pulled Brittney Griner away from her comfort zone in the paint and defensively crowded her beneath the bucket, keeping The Associated Press' Player of the Year from her usual performance. After a sluggish first half the Lady Bears eventually adjusted and schooled Stanford in understanding that Team Baylor is bigger than any one player, even one as talented as Griner.

"We're not the Brittney Griner show," said AP Coach of the Year Kim Mulkey, who had been diagnosed with Bell's palsy just days before the match. "This team is bigger than Brittney."

Senior Terran Condrey stepped up to make big shots, scoring 13 points and putting the zing back in Baylor's game. Defense dynamo Odyssey Sims contributed 11 points and 3 assists, while Jordan Madden added 9 points. Griner finished with 13 points, 9 rebounds, and 2 blocks. With a final score of 59 to 47, the Lady Bears triumphed over the Cardinal to move on to the title game, their primary objective for the entire season.

# STATS, STARS, AND STREAKS

- At 39-0, the Lady Bears owned the longest active winning streak in NCAA Division I women's basketball and were the only undefeated men's or women's team in NCAA Division 1.

- The matchup between Baylor and Stanford featured the nation's top two teams facing off for the third time this season and the 45th time in women's basketball history.

- Baylor advanced to the NCAA Championship title game for the second time in program history.

- Griner completed her ninth game of the season, the first since a 40-minute outing against Texas Tech on Feb. 18.

- Sims played a season-high-tying 40 minutes, played previously against Texas A&M, and marked her third game this season without a turnover.

- Lindsay Palmer received the Elite 89 award for the 2012 NCAA Division I Women's Basketball Championship during the Final Four games.

## BAYLOR 80 VS. NOTRE DAME 61

Tuesday, Apr. 3, 2012, 7:30 pm CT
The Pepsi Center, Denver, Colo.
Attendance: 19,028

### UNFINISHED BUSINESS

Brittney Griner summarized the outcome of the most anticipated game of the season in five words: "The unfinished business is done."

The national championship title belonged to the Lady Bears after a long and arduous journey to the final game of the NCAA tournament. Their overwhelming 80-61 defeat of No. 4 Notre Dame solidified their position in history as the first NCAA Division I basketball team ever to achieve a perfect 40-0 season record.

Notre Dame played to avenge their loss in the 2011 championship finals against Texas A&M, motivated by their season mantra "15:52"—the time remaining in last year's match when the national title slipped from their grasp—as a reminder of their own unfinished business. Notre Dame's Skylar Diggins, considered the top offensive point guard in the country, faced off against Baylor's Odyssey Sims, inarguably the best defensive point guard in collegiate women's basketball. The Fighting Irish made a strong campaign for the win, cutting Baylor's 14-point first-half lead to just six by halftime and narrowing it down to a three-point margin after the break. The Griner Effect foiled yet another opponent as Griner dominated in the paint and finished with 26 points, 13 rebounds, and 5 blocks. Plagued by foul trouble and consistent missed shots, the Notre Dame squad could not provide Diggins with the support she needed to hold back the Lady Bears from a 14-0 run that sealed the fate for a Baylor championship.

Griner received the Most Outstanding Player award for her performance during the tournament, for which she gave credit to her teammates, "All the awards, none of it means anything. If I don't have my team here, we can't get this."

Coach Kim Mulkey deflected the attention away from her own personal achievement of being the only individual to win national championships as a player, an assistant coach, and a head coach: "It's not about me. It's about these kids. They let me coach them. Those kids play hard for me because they know I've got their back."

"This is for Baylor. This is for everything that you can do for a university, to play at the highest level," Mulkey said. "And Baylor is doing that, not just in women's basketball but in all sports."

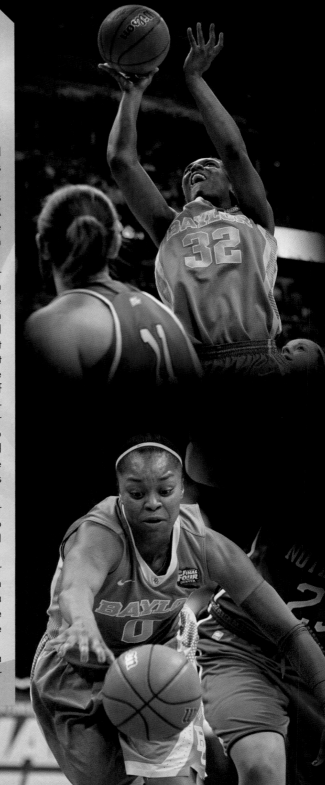

# STATS, STARS, AND STREAKS

- Baylor is the first team in NCAA history to win 40 games in a season. The previous record of 39 wins was reached by both Tennessee (1998) and UConn (2002, 2009, 2010).

- Head Coach Kim Mulkey is now the fifth coach in NCAA history to win more than one national title, joining the likes of Pat Summitt (Tennessee), Geno Auriemma (UConn), Linda Sharp (Southern California), and Tara VanDerveer (Stanford). Mulkey's career record now stands at 338-79.

- Brittney Griner reached 929 points this season, setting a new Big 12 Record and becoming the third-highest single-season total in Baylor history behind Suzie Snider Eppers (1,082 points in 1976-77 and 1,011 in 1974-75).

- Destiny Williams recorded her 29th career double-figure scoring game with a 12-point performance vs. Notre Dame.

- With 19 points, Odyssey Sims recorded her 30th double-digit scoring effort of the season and the 52nd of her career. She tallied double figures in seven straight games to wrap up her sophomore season.

# HOW TO SUPPORT THE LADY BEARS
# AND BAYLOR'S STUDENT ATHLETES

### TIP OFF CLUB

One of the largest collegiate sports clubs in the country, the Tip Off Club exclusively supports Baylor Women's Basketball through annual membership fees.

Members of the Club receive special opportunities to become acquainted with the players and coaches at Club luncheons and invitation-only pregame activities and postgame receptions. Additional benefits include priority parking; access to the Ferrell Center's Stone Room prior to home games; discounted refreshments; the Tip Off Club newsletter; and members-only apparel. For more information or to join the program, visit www.baylor.edu/bearfoundation.

### BAYLOR BEAR FOUNDATION

The Baylor Bear Foundation, established over 70 years ago, is Baylor's primary athletics fundraising organization and supports all 19 Baylor sports. Membership fees for the Baylor Bear Foundation go toward providing scholarship funds for Baylor student athletes and promoting the interests and growth of Baylor Athletics.

Foundation members enjoy a multitude of benefits that include premium seating and parking for basketball and football games, complimentary pre-game meals, access to VIP areas at venues, and the opportunity to purchase priority season, road, and postseason tickets for football, men's basketball, and women's basketball. For more information, visit www.baylor.edu/bearfoundation or send an email to Bear_Foundation@baylor.edu.